Praise for *Marinating Moments*

"Marc Knutson has felt the joys of successes and the pains of failures. He has a balanced story to tell, and this book is his vehicle to reach you, the reader. His life experiences like yours and mine are not always how he imagined; but combined, his experiences are what make a good book. May you glean and enjoy Marc's captivating message."

— Dr. Mike MacIntosh

"I love this book! Marc Knutson has a unique gift for bringing Scripture to everyday life. The Bible happened to real people going about their everyday lives, and Marc helps us slow down and consider their thoughts and emotions. We begin to see and hear the truths of Scripture in a fresh way and realize we have more to learn from the old stories. We constantly need to protect ourselves from thinking we've already learned a lesson. God is still speaking, and He uses new voices like Marc's to help us keep listening. *Marinating Moments* is a good read."

— Terry McNabb, pastor of Calvary Chapel, Portland, OR

"We marinate meat to infuse new flavor by adding enriching seasoning. Marinating takes time, but gives us a little different taste. Marc Knutson takes basic familiar truths and, creatively, gives us a new approach so we can meditate and look at them in fresh ways. He adds meditation questions to each chapter, that we may take time for the marinating to have its full effect."

— Carl Westerlund, director of the School of Ministry, Calvary Chapel, Costa Mesa, CA

MARINATING MOMENTS

IMMERSED in GOD'S RICH WORD

BY

MARC KNUTSON

Published by
Deep River Books
Sisters, Oregon
www.deepriverbooks.com

ISBN: 9781940269788
Library of Congress: 2015960018

Printed in USA
Cover design by Connie Gabbert

The spiritual truths found in the Word of God are the marinade in which human souls should bathe. Immersing ourselves in the enzyme action of God's transforming Word, steeping in the authenticity of His divine reason, will condition and tenderize our hearts for His service. The ultimate result will produce succulent, plump, and savory fruit of the Spirit in and through our lives.

With Much Gratitude

I want to take this time to thank a special friend, LP, whose one word of encouragement after reading parts of the rough draft propelled me toward completing this project.

One word, embedded in one sentence.

One solitary stroke of support gave me the drive, the desire, and the courage to move forward with this project as I teetered in doubt.

That word? "Incredible."

The sentence it was embedded in? "This is incredible, and it will change lives."

Thank you, LP, for the one word that led to so many more!

Contents

Introduction:

Some Thoughts Before You Marinate

I am very excited about this project! I trust that you will share my excitement after you have finished the final chapter and have set the book down and begun to marinate in what you've read. My heartfelt and Spirit-led goal is that your investment of time, weaving your way through these life-altering stories, will enjoy a return of a transformational and a spiritually life-changing experience.

The following pages are intentional attempts to draw you closer to God and strengthen your walk with Him. You could categorize this as a "devotional" book, and there would be nothing wrong with that; however, I believe you will discover that this treatise is more than a mere devotional. It is designed to be *life applicable* and *spiritually transformational*.

The ultimate goal is for you, the reader, to accept a challenge. You will be faced with an opportunity to determine the depth and breadth of your walk with God and to see how the principles contained in these stories can be applied to various areas of your own life.

Reading God's Word is empty if it does not result in life changes and transformational events in the individual believer. Paul wrote to the church at Rome, "And be not conformed to this world: but be ye transformed by the renewing of your mind, that ye may prove what *is* that good, and acceptable, and perfect, will of God." "Renewing" (*anakain sis* in the Greek) means to experience a renewal, a renovation, a complete change for the better.

So as the words of these stories marinate in your thoughts, my hope and ultimate goal is to have the truths penetrate your conscious thoughts and lead to transformational moments—moments that change your spiritual life for the better. Ultimately, I trust that these stories will help you develop an appetite for God, a hunger for His Spirit, and a thirst for the Word!

This compendium consists of simple short stories intertwined with devotional musings and spiritual anecdotes. Some are purposely written in parable form, a very effective teaching/learning device that Jesus used extensively. Some are contemporary or historical in nature, but *all* are designed to be easy reading in a society that struggles to sit long enough to read at all. This entire treatise is designed to encourage you in your journey through life and draw out a spiritual emphasis.

There are enough distractions and attention-stealers in our world that incorporate a sinister common denominator: that of taking our eyes off the prize and our *purpose* in this life! In today's world, it requires constant vigilance and keen concentration to keep Jesus in the focus, or the forefront, of our lives. Therefore, at the conclusion of each story is an exercise to challenge yourself introspectively, or as a group corporately, called "Marinating Moments."

When you're done, it's important that you not just toss the book on the table while mumbling something to the effect of "Well, I did my devotional duty for the day" and run off about your business—leaving the spiritual principles in this book abandoned on the table, gathering dust. Rather, this would be the ideal time to spend *marinating* in thought, allowing the savory enzymes of the Word to draw out the flavorful juices of the spiritual principles that were highlighted in the day's reading. Then allow them to seep deep into your heart and mind, feeling the transformational work of the Holy Spirit as He draws out great flavors in your life.

Whether you read this book for individual meditation or group discussion, the principles illustrated retain a common denominator: they are for everyone.

Writing this compendium was fun, because it allowed me to be creative within the boundaries of my understanding of the Word of God. As a result, I also have the joy of knowing that I can participate in your spiritual growth!

May the Lord richly bless you as you fully *marinate* in His Word!

Marc Knutson

Preface

One of the greatest dining pleasures in life (for anybody but vegetarians) is the flavor of a great cut of meat, be it beef or fish or pork or chicken, which has been immersed in a succulent and juicy marinade. The underlying principle is that the longer the meat steeps in a savory sauce, the more it allows various enzymatic actions to condition, tenderize, infuse, and draw out mouthwatering flavors.

Dr. J. Vernon McGee encouraged his students to "ruminate on the Word, as a cow chews on her cud." A cow chews her food, swallows it, and then brings it back up and chews on it over and over—graphic to be sure, but also highly illustrative and instructive. Like a good ruminant, it is advantageous to read these stories in the morning as a daily devotional and ruminate on the principles throughout the day. The more we steep in the savory sauces of the Word of God, the more it will penetrate our brains and work its way into our hearts. From there, the Word finds the channels to manifest itself through the work of our hands.

As the human being cannot physically survive on a regimen of supplements without sustenance from a balanced diet—the body would wither away and perhaps die—so it is with the Christian soul. It cannot survive on supplements of occasional worship or fellowship, but it requires the meat of the Word of God! I have done my best to provide reflections that are truly "meaty" and nourishing to the soul.

I trust that the questions generated at the end of each chapter will provoke other questions and drive you to seek answers. Some of the stories are parables, some are narratives straight from the Word, and some are more allegorical, but all are practical for enriching our walk with the Lord.

If you are reading this as a home group, which I recommend, take the opportunity to marinate on the Word in healthy group discussion. The benefit of the group environment is that everyone can share his or her thoughts without any feeling of intimidation or reservation based on someone else's position.

During the Marinating Moments at the end of each chapter, you will have the opportunity to personally think the day's reading over or, in a group, to steer your way through a healthy discussion of the principles as they apply to your life or situation.

These stories have been intentionally written in simple, easy-to-understand language. There isn't a lot of "Christianese" here, making the book accessible to more than just veteran Christians. I took great care in specifically keeping it that way, purposefully not lading the stories with overly complicated and ethereal theology, but writing with the intent of maintaining a relational and applicable outcome. You'll find the some of the first-century stories are guilty of anachronism as well: this is intentional, as their lives were not so different from ours! As much as flavor enhancers perk up a meal, let God's Word permeate your soul and perk up your life.

> **AS MUCH AS FLAVOR ENHANCERS PERK UP A MEAL, LET GOD'S WORD PERMEATE YOUR SOUL AND PERK UP YOUR LIFE**

Marinade 1:

What Really Matters

"For who knows what is good for a person in life, during the few and meaningless days they pass through like a shadow? Who can tell them what will happen under the sun after they are gone?"

Ecclesiastes 6:12

A large crowd had gathered at Golgotha, known as the Hill of the Skull, located just outside the walls of Old Jerusalem. They were there to observe what was being hailed as "the Crucifixion of the Century!" Entrepreneurs had wasted no time in printing "I Saw the King of the Jews Crucified" and "Long Live Judas" T-shirts. Some of the chariots cruising the streets of town were emblazoned with bumper stickers that were meant to mock the man's followers, taunting them with "Where's Your King Now?"

One T-shirt and one bumper sticker available at a disgustingly outrageous price: thirty pieces of silver.

Yet, because of the pace of life and all the hustle and bustle of the day, frustration was evident in the onlookers as they scanned their to-do lists. You could hear one exasperated participant say, as he looked over his list of chores, "Um, let's see; I've got to go to the agora for milk and eggs, buy some lamb for dinner, pick up the kids from sling practice, drop off the sacrificial pigeon at the temple, and oh, yeah, there's that crucifixion at Golgotha." With a sigh, he tossed his hands up in the air. "I can't seem to fit it all in one day! Where does the time go?"

One fellow was putting on his freshly purchased T-shirt when he happened to glance upward and noticed that there had been an increase in the cloud cover as the late morning sun began to diminish. Nothing left but shards of light streaking behind the ever-darkening clouds, evidence of a storm brewing on the horizon. Perhaps, because of the intensity of the moment, or the busyness of their lives … but that really didn't matter. It was just another storm.

Was their self-absorption and joy in the eventful day blurring the reality of what was really going on around them?

There were others there also, some not looking very happy, and others certainly not in a reveling mood. For them, to-do lists and gathering storms mean nothing. Their blessed hope, Jesus, the Christ, the carpenter's-son-turned-Messiah, the one they had spent the past three years learning from, was nailed to a Roman cross. The disciples' heavenly hopes suspended by manmade spikes, and like yesterday's newspaper, tossed into the corner like a pile of life's unimportant matters.

Standing there, looking up at the cross, the faithful appeared numbed by the reality and the inescapable finality of death on the cross. They contemplated the undeniable truth of what was happening, and the disciples trembled.

Gripping their hearts were fearful thoughts of being accused of complicity with the "King of the Jews," and perhaps their own eventual capture. Many of them fled for their lives.

One of them was heard yelling, "Let's get out of here! They may take us too!" Therefore, to every nook and cranny of Jerusalem and all of Judea, the disciples of the Messiah fled.

For those who remained, the apostle John and Mary the mother of Jesus and a few of the others … the fear of associating with Jesus didn't really matter.

Fear has a way of over-shadowing the facts. Security is the lack of fear, but fear is the summation of all insecurity.

Maybe the ones who had run weren't even con-

FEAR HAS A WAY OF OVER-SHADOWING THE FACTS. SECURITY IS THE LACK OF FEAR, BUT FEAR IS THE SUM-MATION OF ALL INSECURITY.

centrating on the crucifixion mentally. Their minds were perhaps dwelling on some deep-rooted bitterness they were feeling about their brother, Jesus, who had let them down and totally disappointed them. The questions that doubt, disappointment, and disillusionment can create weigh heavily on human thought.

While their questions weren't uttered, they were written all over their faces. "Where is this great kingdom that He was promising?"

"Why haven't the Romans been put out of business yet?"

"How come He hasn't called a legion of angels to bring Him down from that shame?"

"We trusted Him! Now He's burned us. We'll never trust some-one like Him again."

"We had better skip out, because we're next!"

However, it's important to know that discouragement, disap-pointment, disillusionment, and other "dis" words of that genre are all merely nourishment for the roots of the tree they feed: the tree of bitterness. Toss in a dash of missed expectations, and you have the recipe for another "dis" word—disheartened.

People do that, you know. They allow the vines of bitterness to over-whelm and smother the fruit of the Spirit. The roots of disillusionment and disappointment nourish the fruits of bitterness, and like with most trees, the rotten fruit drops at its base in a disgusting heap.

What a mess.

What a stench.

Do you think they felt the trembling earth beneath their feet as they fled? Do you ever wonder, as they scattered for their lives, if they could hear the ripping sound of the veil coming from the Holy of Holies in the temple?

Can you imagine their facial expressions as they ran past the cemetery and saw graves literally open up? "Isn't that Aunt Mabel walking around? Didn't we just bury her last year?"

Do you think that they noticed the extended darkness as the sun was eclipsed for three hours? With their lives, their careers, their reputations, and their houses at stake … maybe that didn't really matter.

The sky is now darkened. The two convicted criminals, bearing their own crosses on either side of Jesus, are moaning in pain and agony. The jeering mouths of the mob have fallen into silence. There is only the sound of rolling thunder in the distance and the occasional flash of lightning slicing through the eerily blackened sky. The sobbing faithful who remain immediately turn their eyes to Jesus as He is fighting to lift His head to speak. Is He thirsty again? Will they bring Him more of that galling vinegar?

Grimacing in agony, Jesus draws in a deep breath.

Despising the searing pain of a thousand currents racing up His arm like fiery spears, He presses His feet down on the spike, attempting to elevate His torso high enough to inhale so He can speak. Pushing up just enough to allow the last molecules of air left in His lungs to pass over His royal vocal cords, He declares one final edict from the throne of God to His creation called man.

With regal validation, the authoritative words "It is finished" tumble out and begin their heralding journey, bounding down the halls of time. It was then and there that Jesus allowed His Spirit to leave the tent known as His body and ascend back to the throne room of God.

WITH REGAL VALIDATION, THE AUTHORITATIVE WORDS "IT IS FINISHED" TUMBLE OUT AND BEGIN THEIR HERALDING JOURNEY, BOUNDING DOWN THE HALLS OF TIME.

Have you ever wondered what really mattered to them, to the disciples and the crowds, at that time? Can you picture the people running, fleeing with cupped hands over their ears to stop the haunting echoes of "it is finished"?

As you read this, I challenge you to stop in your rat-race tracks for a moment.

Be still.

There now, can you hear it? It's loud, as if shouted from the cross, but whispered in your heart, "*It is finished!*"

The cry remains pretty loud, despite the centuries. Even though time serves as a damper, and for the most part fades messages, yet even today you can still hear those words. You can still hear them echoing through the canyons of time and ricocheting off the walls of history— God's promise from the cross: "It is finished!"

But, we ask, what is "finished"?

For starters, here are just some of many possible answers: The grip of spiritual death on man's eternity. The debt that man owes God as the result of sin. The sentence (what is owed) of eternal hell, with no parole or time off for good behavior. Frankly, that's what is finished.

Do you think those words *mattered* to them, really?

> *"Therefore I tell you, do not worry about your life, what you will eat or drink; or about your body, what you will wear. Is not life more than food, and the body more than clothes?*

Matthew 6:25

Marinating Moments

Oftentimes, an item that is immersed and marinating in a great sauce needs to be turned over. So, before we complete the story, let's take a moment to marinate on what we've read so far:

1. What gets in your way to prevent you from noticing what is really going on around you, or even stops you from time with the Lord?

2. Discuss practical ways to keep your appointment with your Savior every day or more often. Share your ideas with the group.

3. Meditate on and discuss with the group what Jesus "finished" in your life. What would you have been sentenced for if not for Jesus's sacrifice?

Marinade 2:

What Really Matters: Part Deux

"When he had received the drink, Jesus said, 'It is finished.'
With that, he bowed his head and gave up his spirit."

John 19:30

Now, let's pick up the balance of the story as we conclude it. Imagine standing at the base of the cross and hearing the words of Jesus, "It is finished," and wondering, as we have already asked, what is finished? All that mattered to them was that He was there to set up His kingdom, and now the Romans had disposed of Him.

Or was it the scheming, religiously blinded Pharisees who were responsible for hanging Him there?

Now He's proclaiming what? His life is finished? His ministry has ended?

What is He talking about?

Even if His enemies stood there for centuries, cupping their hands over their ears, shouting "La-la-la-la" to themselves, they could not block the haunting decree from Calvary, the Hill of the Skull.

We all know that the blame cannot be placed on any one government or religious group but squarely on a race! The race called "human." The base nature of humankind drove the spikes into His body, but His own love for humanity held Him there.

> **THE BASE NATURE OF HUMANKIND DROVE THE SPIKES INTO HIS BODY, BUT HIS OWN LOVE FOR HUMANITY HELD HIM THERE.**

Those who remained at Golgotha were standing in awe, having to process the meaning of His final words. Make sure, though, that you take note of something that happened.

God made sure that we didn't miss it.

After Jesus's words freed man from the grip of sin, spiritual death, and the stranglehold of the law, he declared, "Father, into thy hands I commend my spirit." Jesus had told Pontius Pilate earlier that "No man can take my life except I give it!" Life didn't just ebb out of Jesus: He surrendered it.

Christ chose to die that we might live.

It is here that we discover that perhaps we take life too seriously!

The hustle and bustle of our daily routines!

The extreme emphasis placed on money.

The overimportance placed on the lives of movie stars!

> **CHRIST CHOSE TO DIE THAT WE MIGHT LIVE.**

The overemphasis on sports figures and their multimillion salaries. The idolization of successful sinners.

So much of our lives have become consumed, eaten up by and absorbed with the insignificant cares of this world, and not with, well … what really matters.

Little had Mary known yesterday that in just twenty-four hours she would be assisting Joseph of Arimathea and others in anointing the corpse of her boy with embalming fluids, nor did she realize that Jesus would assign her to the care of His friend, John.

Nevertheless, it was in the glow of the Sunday morning dawn that the most amazing series of events occurred. Perhaps it was the vibrations of the stone rolling aside during the earthquake that awoke both Mary, the mother of Jesus, and Mary Magdalene. Or perhaps it was their memories of His curiously haunting words that flooded their minds: "On the third day I will rise again." For some reason, they mutually agreed to go to the sepulcher together.

As they drew near to the tomb that morning laden with embalming oils and myrrh, they had doubts about the integrity of the waxen security seal placed on the tomb entrance. Was He still in there? Was their marvelous sense of women's intuition picking up on what Jesus had been teaching? If so—logically, He shouldn't be there!

Shortly, after their personally guided tour of the vacant sepulcher by an angel, Mary was instructed to run and get the other disciples and especially Peter.

Don't miss that!

The angel specifically named Peter! Notice, he didn't immediately call for John, the disciple whom Jesus loved. Nor Thomas, the one who had doubts. Not even James, Jesus's half-brother … but Peter!

Peter?

The one who denied Jesus three times in one morning, before breakfast? That Peter? The one who vowed that they would have to get through him before they could get to Jesus, and then cowered away from confrontation by a girl?

THE DISAPPOINTER ELEVATED BY THE DISAPPOINTEE.

That same Peter?

Yes! That Peter!

I'm reminded of a scene in *Star Wars*. Darth Vader looks at his Death Star commander and says, "You have failed me for the last time," then kills him for his failure. However Jesus, the resurrected Jesus, calls for Peter the man. Not for his head. The man who let him down is going to be raised up. The man who wept bitterly in the disappointment of forsaking Jesus is now being called upon by the disappointed. The disappointer elevated by the disappointee.

But perhaps we need to look at this from another angle. Could Jesus really have been disappointed, if in fact he knew all along that

Peter was going to fail him? Could Jesus be disappointed in *you*, knowing all along that you were going to do what you did?

What a glimpse we get of God and the dawning of things that really matter!

We get a glimpse of a God who doesn't punish you because you failed.

We get a glimpse of a God who doesn't hold grudges because you denied Christ, not once, not twice, but three times, while cleverly cloaked by the early morning darkness.

We get a glimpse of a God who forgives quicker than you can say, "Please forgive me!"

We get a glimpse of a God who originated the term, "No worries."

We get a glimpse of a God of second, third, fourth, and seventy-times-seven chances! In fact, when you look up "forgiveness" in a heavenly dictionary, you see a picture of Jesus.

The angel said, "Go tell the others that the risen Christ wants to meet with them. He wants to talk with them about, well … what really matters."

You mean the very same Jesus who just three days earlier handed over His spirit to God?

Yes, the very same.

The Universal God, resurrected among men, is inviting them to share breakfast with Him on the beach.

So, what have you discovered about what *really* matters in your life?

Your bills?

Your car?

Your yard?

Your house?

Your income?

Your looks?

Notice, those are all temporal and material things!

Someone asked the multibillionaire John D. Rockefeller the question, "How much money is enough?" His answer was, "One more dollar than I have." He therefore would never have enough, no matter how many billions he had.

Where should most of our concentrated time be spent? Worrying about money? Well, money rates pretty highly in most of our minds, but … does that really matter?

Dwelling on an uncertain future? That ranks high also, but aren't we told that God has our future planned?

Perhaps you place a high priority on making sure you are all tied up in emotional knots about your life.

Well, here's what Jesus thought, and taught, about the matter. Matthew 6:25–27:

> Therefore I tell you, do not worry about your life, what you will eat or drink; or about your body, what you will wear. Is not life more than food, and the body more than clothes? Look at the birds of the air; they do not sow or reap or store away in barns, and yet your heavenly Father feeds them. Are you not much more valuable than they? Can any one of you by worrying add a single hour to your life?

The apostle Paul has an answer too. He wrote in 1 Corinthians 15:1–11:

> Now, brothers and sisters, I want to remind you of the gospel I preached to you, which you received and on which you have taken your stand. By this gospel you are saved, if you hold firmly to the word I preached to you. Otherwise, you have believed in vain. For what I received I passed on to you as of first importance: that Christ died for our sins according to the Scriptures, that he was buried, that he was raised on the third day according to the Scriptures, and that he appeared to Cephas, and then to the Twelve. After that, he appeared to more than five hundred of the brothers and sisters at the same time, most of whom

are still living, though some have fallen asleep. Then he appeared to James, then to all the apostles, and last of all he appeared to me also, as to one abnormally born.

For I am the least of the apostles and do not even deserve to be called an apostle, because I persecuted the church of God. But by the grace of God I am what I am, and his grace to me was not without effect. No, I worked harder than all of them—yet not I, but the grace of God that was with me. Whether, then, it is I or they, this is what we preach, and this is what you believed.

WHAT MATTERS, REALLY, IS WHAT REALLY MATTERS *IN GOD'S EYES.*

Why Jesus did it is what really matters!

There it is—what really matters is the gospel of Jesus the Christ!

What matters, really, is what really matters *in God's eyes.* It almost seems too simple. Jesus was executed, buried, and resurrected. What really matters is what happened on the cross ... and three days later: No more, no less!

We can't ignore it. Golgotha lies along the timeline of man's history like a jewel, a brilliantly compelling diamond, so big that men trip over it and demand its removal. No wonder the apostle Paul called it the "core of the gospel" (1 Corinthians 15:3–4).

Perhaps the cross is nothing new to you. You've worn it, you've seen it, you've read about it, you may have even prayed to it. But do you know it? Do you know *why* so much emphasis is placed on it? *Because* of the cross, *because* of what happened on the cross, and *because* of the events that happened right after it ... because of the whole story God is telling, the cross is what really matters.

The story is about a cross and a tomb, which remain empty and abandoned, respectively.

However, don't let the emptiness reflect sadness, because the Bible tells us, "For the joy that was set before Him, He endured the shame of the cross" (Hebrew 12:2b).

> THE EMPTY CROSS AND THE UNOCCUPIED TOMB ARE WHAT NO OTHER FAITH ON EARTH CAN PROVIDE.

The cross may be vacant; the tomb may not be hosting a corpse. However, therein is the good news for man! The empty cross and the unoccupied tomb are what no other faith on earth can provide.

Our hope of eternity rests on the resurrected Christ ... that's what really matters.

#

It is well past the events of that horrific day on the Mount of the Skull. The earth hasn't trembled like that since.

The once-darkened sky has now cleared to a crystal blue.

The confused temple workers are busy repairing the torn veil.

The cemetery workers are scratching their heads as they return the sod back over the opened graves, questioning among themselves the legality or the authority they have to reseal empty graves.

Everything seems to be returning to normal in Jerusalem. No one appears to be asking, "Whatever happened to those living testimonies of God's miracles, the walking, once-dead people?"

Although there are those who have a quiet confidence to the contrary: Jerusalem will never be the same again. God made a house call on man and chose Jerusalem as the place.

There are those who missed it.

There are those who refused it.

However, there are those who have received His call and confidently walk in peace and the hope of His return.

#

Stop and take a look at the things of value in your life. What really matters to you? Do you live with that hope? Do you live with the hope of His return?

What really matters is what you have done about Jesus! One day, as you stand before the judgment seat of Christ, you won't be bragging about your mansions, your fat IRAs, or your antique car collections. Rather, you'll be praising God and sharing what really matters: your work for the kingdom's sake in the timeline called "your life."

"For I delivered unto you first of all that which I also received, how that Christ died for our sins according to the scripture, and that he was buried, and that he rose again the third day according to the scriptures."

1 Corinthians 15:3–4 (KJV)

Marinating Moments

1. What really matters in your life today? That big house? The shiny car? Be honest with yourself and with God, who knows your heart.

2. Are your actions lining up with the five "Glimpses of God"? Have you received His forgiveness? Are you living in the knowledge of His grace?

3. How much influence would you say the world has over your thinking and behaviors? Are you living to please the world or the Savior? Would you say this world or eternity has the bigger pull on your heart?

Marinade 3:

The Garden of Discontent

*"If they obey and serve him, they will spend the rest of their
days in prosperity and their years in contentment."*

Job 36:11

My drooping eyelids were tapping out Morse code messages to my
brain in rapid succession. Every dot and dash was encouraging me to
put the book down and go to sleep. It was difficult for me to comply,
as I was so enjoying the imagination of James Hilton and his descrip-
tion of the hidden paradise of Shangri-La. His depiction of the idyllic
settings and utopian splendor was captivating.

However, it was a useless struggle of the flesh over the mind—the
flesh was winning without much of a fight. I felt slumber begin to creep
in over me like fog shrouding a rocky coastline. Setting the book on
the nightstand, I barely felt the release as I yielded to my tiredness and
the wacky day. Switching off the lamp, I think I was out before the last
photons of light were swallowed up by the darkness of the room.

Sometime later in the night, I am not quite sure when, I was
aroused from my deep sleep by an apparent disturbance outside. My
eyes probed to check the time, but the only glimpse they got was that
it was about blur o'clock in the morning. I decided to lie motionless; perhaps I could hear the sound again. Then, within moments,
it happened once more. I wasn't clear on what was going on outside,

but there indeed was a commotion of some sort, as evidenced by the cacophony filling my ears. The voices were loud and getting louder. I couldn't lie there any longer. If I were to get any sleep at all, I was going to have to take some action.

In my drowsy fogginess, I stumbled down the hall, grabbed the prepositioned baseball bat (placed in the hallway for just such an occasion), and continued toward the back door. With my bat at the ready and all my senses starting to come online, I felt emboldened enough to ease up to the door, slightly retract the drape, and try to catch a glimpse of what was going on outside. What I saw amazed me. In fact, I am not quite sure how to express in words what I saw, because my own eyes were struggling with the scene.

Electing not to flood the yard with the porch light, I reached for the doorknob and quietly unlocked the deadbolt. In one stealthy and swift move, I powerfully jerked on the door handle, swinging the door open, and leapt out on the deck.

> INSTANTLY, EVERYTHING FELL SILENT. ALL THE COMMOTION VANISHED ON THE SPOT. ALL I COULD HEAR WERE CRICKETS CRICKETING IN THE DISTANCE.

Instantly, everything fell silent. All the commotion vanished on the spot. All I could hear were crickets cricketing in the distance. Scanning the yard in the creepy quiet, I saw a thousand tiny pinpoints of lights scattered about, occasionally flickering. It was as though hundreds of fireflies had graced my backyard with their warm glow. I knelt down to get a closer look at these emissions of light, and discovered they weren't lights at all—but sets of eyes. Eerily, they were all staring at me, occasionally blinking their eyes. From some place farther back in the yard, I heard a conciliatory but muffled voice mumble, "Uh-oh, busted!"

"Who is that?" I exclaimed.

Nothing.

"Who said that?" Still, no response.

"Come on now, speak up." I scanned the yard in a left-to-right pattern, from the grass to the flower beds to the trees. I saw no one. Then I caught on to what was happening. It finally dawned on me that I had just wandered into the middle of a skirmish. A battle for supremacy in the yard, for the yard, and by the yard. I had achieved my goal, to catch the intruders in the act—although who I caught were not intruders at all. It was my own yard in a huge territorial turf war.

The lawn, the flower beds, the hanging plants, even the trees were all having at it. I was quite embarrassed for them. I decided to turn on the porch light and expose them all to their humiliation. Walking along the deck, I spoke first: "Okay, what is this all about anyway? I am trying to get some sleep here, and you are all making such a ruckus. You ought to be ashamed of yourselves." I thought maybe tossing out a few chiding remarks would help them see their own foolish behavior.

Mustering my best parental tone of voice, I barked out, "Okay, I'll ask again, who started this mess?" I first looked at the two clumps of grass over near the corner of the yard, whose blades were still in a mid-parry defensive posture. All they could do was stare at me, then blink, then stare some more. Mouths gaping open, they didn't have an answer for me.

Crabgrass broke the stalemate and spoke up first. "I don't like my spot in the yard, and this guy makes it worse," he whined as he pointed his unsheathed blade at the Bermuda grass that served as his fencing competition. Crabgrass continued, "He so annoys me, touting his rich green blades and that nose-in-the-air attitude because of that high-falutin' name: 'Bermuda'."

Waving his blade in the air, he continued, "Come on, he's no better than me! Why does he get such a fancy name, and I'm stuck with 'crabgrass'? That's not fair, and if he even looks at me again, why I'll . . ."

"Oh, stop it! Get a clue why you may be called 'crab' grass," I interjected, not allowing him to finish his sentence. "You're merely proving why you deserve your name."

> IT FELT GOOD TO MOW HIM DOWN IN MID-SENTENCE. I WAS FORTUNATE THAT I'D GOTTEN OUT HERE WHEN I DID. ANOTHER STERN LOOK FROM ME, AND BOTH CRABGRASS AND BERMUDA CROSSED THEIR BLADES ACROSS THEIR CHESTS AND TURNED THEIR BACKS TO EACH OTHER.

Bermuda began to defend himself. "I didn't ask for this to happen." I did detect a slight aristocratic accent as he spoke. "I was merely minding my own place in the yard, enjoying a spot of tea. Furthermore, as far as proxemics goes, *he's* too close to *me*. He doesn't keep his creepy rhizomes to himself. His roots want to tangle with mine. I've had it! I simply cannot continue to live in such abhorrent conditions. I demand to have a different spot in the yard. Besides, I've been here since the yard was first planted. I deserve a good spot in the yard. He's a new guy, and . . ."

"Don't even get started, Bermuda." It felt good to mow him down in mid-sentence. I was fortunate that I'd gotten out here when I did. Another stern look from me, and both Crabgrass and Bermuda crossed their blades across their chests and turned their backs to each other. "I'll come back to you two clods in a moment. I first need to check out what else is going on."

Bumping my head on one of the hanging planters, I heard a voice yell, "Hey, watch where you're going down there! We're fragile up here. One careless bump, and we'll all come crashing down."

Rubbing my head near the spot that had glanced the basket, I looked up. "Who you snapping at, fella?" I asked the little community of snapdragons hovering overhead in the planter that was still slightly spinning and twirling. One of the dragons in the center of the planter said, "Uh-oh, I think I am going to get airsick." The other stalks quickly leaned away from the nauseated one. Reaching for the planter, I stopped its swaying motion and said in a soft voice, "No one is going to get airsick."

"Well, we don't belong up here in a hanging planter," said the spokesdragon of the group. "We're supposed to be down there, in the flower beds!"

As I scanned across the landscape of the yard, the garden pandemonium

"WELL, WE DON'T BELONG UP HERE IN A HANG-ING PLANTER," SAID THE SPOKESDRAGON OF THE GROUP. "WE'RE SUPPOSED TO BE DOWN THERE, IN THE FLOWER BEDS!"

erupted again. All the plants were talking and yelling at each other . . . and at me. I wasn't far from the pansies, who were complaining that the snapdragons were being mean and snapping at them.

The violets were shrinking away from the fray. One spoke up, claiming that they didn't want to get involved.

The crocuses were croaking about the suffocating size of the pot they were planted in.

The impatiens were snippy. The baby's breath was being cared for by the widow's tears.

It was unbelievable; my yard was out of control. It was filled with unhappy plants. All the commotion, all the noise, all the complaining going on at one time meant that no one was listening. Everyone was flapping their stamens. Except of course the cornstalks—they always carried smug grins because their motto was, "We're all ears."

The dandelions were lying low. They crouched throughout the yard, all the while appearing to be quite dandy. However, I wasn't fooled by their sunny dispositions and smiling faces, because I knew about them. Their destructive culture was an act of surface deception and subterranean terror. On the surface they were smiling, and all the while choking grass roots under the cover of sod.

It seemed as if everything out there was trying to get my attention. They wanted me to do something about their situations, coming at me from all sorts of directions. No one was happy. At this point, I wasn't either. I just wanted to go back to bed.

> IT SEEMED AS IF EVERY-
> THING OUT THERE WAS
> TRYING TO GET MY ATTEN-
> TION. THEY WANTED ME
> TO DO SOMETHING ABOUT
> THEIR SITUATIONS, COMING
> AT ME FROM ALL SORTS OF
> DIRECTIONS.

For some reason, I'm not sure why, I decided to stroll down the garden path that led to the center of the yard, a promenade among the flora. That's when I heard a giggle, and then a voice said, "He's so handsome." I wasn't sure where that came from, but out of the corner of my eye I detected some movement. That's when I noticed that a tall, mature, purple gladiola was leaning over to an equally tall and mature red gladiola. "I love the way he saunters down the garden path, so confident and assured. Tee-hee," continued the purple gladiola as her huge eyes followed my every move.

"I'm right here," I blurted out in embarrassment. "I can hear you. Why are you saying that?"

I barely got my question asked. The purple gladiola was just about to respond when we were interrupted. "Aw man, there go those annoying glads, kissing up to the owner again. '*Isn't he so handsome*,'" mocked the bitterroot. "Bah, those glads are as phony as a four-leafed clover. If they had hands they'd be all over him!"

"Hey!" yelled the clover from the corner of the yard. "Don't pick on us, we're just minding our own business over here."

Bitterroot was about to say something else, but this time it was my turn to lop off his reply like finely sharpened shears. Reaching

> BITTERROOT WAS ABOUT TO
> SAY SOMETHING ELSE, BUT
> THIS TIME IT WAS MY TURN
> TO LOP OFF HIS REPLY LIKE
> FINELY SHARPENED SHEARS.

down and grabbing a blossom from a nearby flag plant, I tossed it in the air and watched it land in a heap. "Fifteen yard penalty," I snipped while pointing at the bitterroot, "for unnecessary bitterness and unhappiness! The penalty will be assessed on the ensuing spring planting and will move you fifteen yards further back toward the fence!"

"Aw, c'mon man," whined Bitterroot, with his roots crossed in front of his chest. "All I was saying was the truth. Those glads are always kissing up to you and thinking you're all that! Gimme a break!" I have to say that Bitterroot was tenaciously holding his position.

Gladys, the purple gladiola, spoke first, "Well, Mr. Bitterroot, if it's all the same to you, we are always glad to see him coming out into the garden. We know that he is usually out here helping us, cleaning weeds out from between us, caring for and nurturing his garden." Tossing a wink up at me she added, "We love him." That was a little too much mushiness even for my liking.

"See!" screamed Bitterroot, "there she goes again, getting all chummy-chummy with you. It makes me sick! As a matter of fact, I hear that things are better in the neighbor's yard. The grass is greener over there. I hear that they eat from better-watered and fertilized soil. It's just way better over there!"

"That's all hearsay," I retorted through a saddened countenance. "Besides, I'm not flagging you because of what you said to Gladys," I chided Bitterroot, "I'm flagging *all* of you because you are always complaining and groaning about something."

Stooping down to get face-to-face with the deep-set pair of eyes that were almost buried in the huge, white-blossomed face of the bitterroot, I continued in an exaggeratedly mocking tone, "I don't get this; they always get that; I'm in the wrong spot; I can't believe I get treated like that."

My words dripped with sarcasm. Standing up, I continued to scold Bitterroot and the entire yard, not in a mocking but a serious tone. "Face it, you always act the way you are acting now: smugly crossing your branches, pushing out those pouty buds. I mean, look at your body language. It screams bad attitude! Bad attitudes, that's what this flag is for! This entire yard has a bad attitude!"

"May I have a word?" came a voice from behind me.

I FOCUSED IN ON THE VOICE AND DISCOVERED THAT IT WAS THE ROSE OF SHARON ASKING ME FOR PERMISSION TO SPEAK.

Spinning around to follow the voice, I heard again, "May I have a moment to address my neighbors?"

I focused in on the voice and discovered that it was the rose of Sharon asking me for permission to speak.

"Well," I quipped, "only if what you have to add will be positive and not just sappier complaints."

His eyes met mine. I felt that our optic nerves had been surgically connected. "Okay," I said in a low, dulcet tone, the result of my mesmerized consciousness. "Have at it, and may I add, good luck!" From my perspective, he was in a thorny predicament.

Like an orator, he began to address the entire rebellious yard. "When he planted you, he planted you in particular places to do particular jobs. Look, snappies, you grow tall and lean and reach high for the sun. Now, look at your neighbors: they are short and not very heat tolerant. He placed you next to them so they could benefit from the shading you give them in the hot summer months. You are where you are for a reason. So bloom where you have been planted. Your only responsibility, your only duty, is to be the best of who you were made to be, right where you are, and not to try to be something else. Trust in him who planted you there. Live by faith and allow that faith to grow into deep, healthy roots. The seeds of doubt and discouragement find root in the soils of ignorance. However, faith grows when it is properly watered, properly fed, and able to receive plenty of light. In return, faith produces hearty fruit—but the noxious weeds of doubt, disillusionment, and even discouragement can creep in and choke out vital nutrients. The only fruit that develops from that are the tangled roots of bitterness."

Now that he was in stride, he had their attention, all of them. "Look," he continued as he pointed to the plants strung on wire along the fence line. "Look at the Berry Brothers over there. There's Rasp,

Boysen, Blue, and of course, below them, their brother Straw." The Berry Brothers all had big grins now that the attention was on them. One even mocked doffing his hat to the audience.

Without even as much as a cue, Rasp Berry interrupted the rose of Sharon and began to address the entire yard. "Yup, I like my spot in the yard," rasped Rasp Berry.

Boysen followed up on Rasp's heels. "Boy, it's cool to be here," his mellow voice flowed through his wide-goateed grin.

Rose looked at Blue and shrugged his branches. He said, in a resigning tone, "Go ahead, I won't stop you."

Blue grinned wide. "That's cool, Daddio. You cats all need to chill and dial it down a few octaves before you all wind up recycled in the compost bin. Gellin's cool. You dig?" Unfortunately, mostly blank stares and the occasional blink ensued.

I saw Straw's mouth open. He was about to add a few tendrils to the conversation, but Rose sliced him off before he got started.

"Okay everyone, look here, look at me," he commanded, waving his leaves in a fashion that drew everyone's attention to his face. Pivoting in a circle to ensure that he had the entire yard's eyes on himself, he continued, "Look at the example that the Berry Brothers show us. He has planted them in good, rich soil. Their roots wiggle down and retrieve abundant nutrients. He administers an appropriate amount of water, and they've been planted unobstructed from the sun's full rays."

So far so good. The peace was holding, and Rose maintained everyone's attention.

"As they told you, they are happy where they've been planted. As a result, they produce good, hearty fruit. What do we learn from that?" Rose asked rhetorically. Good thing too, because based on the stares and the occasional blinks, apparently no one was anxious to answer. Even the johnnie jump-ups sought to lay low.

The rose continued, "We learn that with good food, ample water, and a proper place in the sun, we can all produce healthy fruit and help our neighbor at the same time, right? And, most of all, it's all for the owner's pleasure."

> "WE LEARN THAT WITH GOOD FOOD, AMPLE WATER, AND A PROPER PLACE IN THE SUN, WE CAN ALL PRODUCE HEALTHY FRUIT AND HELP OUR NEIGHBOR AT THE SAME TIME, RIGHT? AND, MOST OF ALL, IT'S ALL FOR THE OWNER'S PLEASURE."

As the rose's words faded out, I heard a short cooing sound coming from Gladys and her red friend. I shot an "if looks could kill" glance at them, which caused them to shrink back and cover their lips with their petals.

Their cowering made me realize that I had been getting a bit wound up myself. It was late, I was tired and cranky, but I shouldn't have yelled at Bitterroot like that—it just wasn't right. So, to the entire backyard I said, "Sorry I got all fired up there, folks. Please forgive me; I allowed my emotions to overwhelm me."

In unison, I could hear a chorus of voices mumbling things like "that's all right" and "no worries." Bitterroot spoke up in a lilting voice: "Does that mean I don't have to move back?"

"No," I replied sharply, "you still have to pay the penalty. You brought that on yourself, but what it does mean is that I apologize for raising my voice at you guys."

"Oh," replied Bitterroot, back to his mocking tone of voice, "they always get preferential treatment . . ." Catching himself in midsentence, he humbly placed a leaf over his lips, stopped speaking, and embarrassedly said, "Oops, sorry," dragging the word "sorry" out with extra emphasis.

> I SIMPLY SMILED AS THE YARD LAUGHED AND IMMEDIATELY STARTED ARGUING AGAIN.

I simply smiled as the yard laughed and immediately started arguing again.

It was then that I heard a voice over the others. It was loud and trying to get my attention. I finally was able to hush the bickering yard into a long enough quiet to hear the voice calling me again, but this voice wasn't from within my yard.

"Yoo-hoo! Yoo-hoo! May I chime in with my two petals' worth?"

Finally, I saw where it was coming from. A single eye was peeking at me through the cragged slits of the rickety old fence that separated us from the neighbor's yard.

I called out to the eye that was peeping through the fence. "Are you trying to get our attention?" I asked.

"Yes, yes, it's me." She was tall, thin, and sported a nice beard.

"What's your name?" I inquired, thinking down deep that I was never going to get back to bed.

"Iris," she replied. "Look, we on our side of the fence have been listening to you guys for a long time. We want to assure you that things are not any better over here than on your side of the fence. As members of the Greener on the Other Side of the Fence Society, your arguments are similar to ours. Some on our side of the fence think that living on your side would offer richer and more rewarding opportunities than our side. We spend an awful lot of time in that same debate. But when I hear you guys arguing over the same issues, I am convinced that you are no better off over there than we are here." Iris had everyone's ears. You could hear a thistle drop.

"We are learning to be content here with what we have, and with where we've been placed—well, most of us at least. Sadly, we do have a few rhubarbs here and there ourselves." Silence prevailed.

"Hear, hear," chanted a pansy on our side. "Hear, hear," chanted the entire bed of brilliant yellow-and-purple pansies that formed a beautiful border along the deck area. "It takes a while," said the spokespansy, "but we have learned to be content and to bloom where we're planted, just like our neighbors in the other flower bed. They never say a word."

"Aw, shut up, pansies, you always have some phony outlook on life that makes you think that you're so hoity-toity," complained the crab-grass. "Besides, your supposedly content neighbors are mums. They never say anything anyway. Don't try to pull something over on us!"

Stopping only long enough to take a breath, he jumped back in. "You don't have it so tough, you know. You get food and water and a little pruning, but the owner always takes care of you. Now we crabgrass types, well, when we get too hoity-toity, we get the lawn-mower cutting us down to size. Hey, so we drink a little too much of Bermuda's water—and maybe our roots get a wee bit tangled from time to time—but that's who we are! That's how we were made. So just pipe down and keep your pansy-style rose-colored windows to yourselves!"

"Well," huffed the impatiens, not known for enduring a squabble or taking a barb from the crabgrass, "of all the nerve to talk to those poor pansies that way! Life is short, too short to take yourselves so seriously."

I was in awe of the pansies as they continued, "It's a frightening world out there on the other side of the fence—you think it's greener, but in reality … well, let's say that it is important to recognize where we are placed in the overall scope of this existence we call life. We must see that it is not all toil and labor. Life is not getting up in the morning, rushing to work, expending all our energies to leave nothing for our family or home or ourselves. Life begins when the quitting bell rings. If you live to work, then you won't enjoy life at all …"

"Ah, sheesh, pansies, impatiens, I have no place for you!" bemoaned the crabgrass.

I WANT TO LET YOU IN ON A SECRET HERE—OUR SIDE LOOKS LIKE GREENER GRASS, BUT DON'T BE MIS-LED. OUR OWNER HIRES A SERVICE THAT COMES IN MONTHLY AND SPRAYS A LAYER OF A VEGETABLE-OIL-BASED GREEN PAINT.

"As I was saying," continued the pansy with her leaves crossed and her horizontally squint-ing eyes boring holes into the crab, "If you work to live—then, by pacing yourself, you'll leave some energy at the end of the day, when life really starts. You'll look less for greener grass in other yards and concentrate more on living this life, right where you were planted."

"Hear, hear," chimed in the other pansies.

Iris jumped back in. "One final thought. I want to let you in on a secret here—our side looks like greener grass, but don't be misled. Our owner hires a service that comes in monthly and sprays a layer of a vegetable-oil-based green paint. It's merely a fraudulent cosmetic deception to make you think our side of the fence is greener than your side. Don't fall for it; beneath the green paint, we are all just like you!"

"Wow, we've been duped," growled the dogwoods.

Iris's two petals' worth hung in the air, and all was peaceful, serene, and enjoyably quiet. It was the first time since all this began that nothing in the yard said a thing. The crickets even began cricketing again. I had a fleeting thought that perhaps I could retire to my bed again and finish the night.

But then the dwarf peaches broke the silence, "Yeah, whatever," whined a dwarf peach, puncturing a hole in the short-lived silence. "I'm still upset that Cling appears more desirable and has a smaller pit!"

The shattered tranquility triggered a cascading effect as the entire yard was back at it again. Bing, one of the cherries, fell right in step, "Aw c'mon now, talk about the pits! Proportionately, speaking of fruit-to-pit ratios, my pit is larger than yours! You whine too much for a dwarf."

"All right you two," I barked, which caused the dogwoods to growl again.

From the corner of my eye, I could see the rose of Sharon shaking his head in amazement. The Berry Brothers continued to grin with joy, but everyone else was back into the fray.

I tossed my hands in the air in disgust and frustration, turned and headed back toward the door. The rose of Sharon added a few consoling words as I walked by him. "Don't be too angry with them," he said as if he were the chief representative of the whole yard. "They don't realize what they're doing. I'll speak to them further. Give them a chance and don't rototill them into the compost bin."

With pursed lips, and doing my best to maintain my composure in my cranky state, I looked down at him. The look on the rose's face caused me to almost immediately reconsider my irritability. "I won't do anything too rash—but speak to them, okay? Take over here. Bring peace to the yard and let me get back to sleep." His deeply concerned face immediately turned into a beaming smile as I stepped up on the deck.

When I reached the door, I stopped as I heard Rose speak up and instantly quiet the din. "May I have your attention, please! Everyone listen up." A hush fell across the garden as Rose spoke. "The point of discontentment has been made very well here tonight. Nevertheless, I have to say that contentment is something we have to learn. We have to learn to be content no matter where we have been planted. It is a process, but it's a process in self-discipline. We must learn that we are where we are for a reason, perhaps a much larger one than we can understand. Once we learn that, we can bloom beyond our, or anybody's, expectations."

The last thing I remember is looking back and smiling inwardly as I saw that the eyes and ears of the entire rebellious yard were on the rose. He had their attention and apparently their respect.

And now, I told myself, *I'll get some sleep.*

#

It took me a few moments to realize that the small but insistent tugging on my elbow was my wife, gently trying to awaken me. "Morning," she whispered as she nuzzled her lips close to my ear.

Lifting my head from the pillow, I glanced at the clock to see that it was later than I usually slept, even for a weekend. "Morning," I replied with the heavy fog of grogginess surrounding my head.

"You tossed and turned a lot last night," she said as she was putting on her robe.

Rubbing my face and my eyes, I lay there trying to make sense of what had happened last night. "You know," I said, "I am not sure what happened. I think I heard a noise and got up to check it out and . . ."

"No, you didn't get out of bed at all. I was awakened by all your stirring. I didn't get a wink of sleep, so I know you never got up. Perhaps you were having a bad dream?" Pointing to my nightstand she asked, "When did you bring that in?"

I looked over at the nightstand but didn't see what she was talking about. I did see the book I had placed there, but that was all.

Propping myself up on my right elbow, I could see that lying behind the clock on the nightstand was a flower. Sunlight was streaming in through the window, but I still couldn't make out what it was. I reached out to examine it. "It looks like a rose of Sharon," my wife said as she tied the sash of her robe around her waist. "Why didn't you place it in some water?"

Staring at it, I noticed the slight dripping of sap from under one of the extended fronds. I replied, "I don't even remember bringing this in. I don't know how it got here."

I dressed and followed my wife out, carrying the rose, which drooped wilted and lifeless.

The living room drapes were open wide, permitting shafts of sunlight to beam into the house and allowing me to see the entire backyard as I sauntered toward the kitchen. It was weird to look out there and see all the plants I'd had such a strange dream about, but then I saw something, or at least thought I saw something, that caused me to stop suddenly in my tracks.

"What's wrong, honey?" my wife asked as I remained in place, holding the rose and just staring outside. She came over and began rubbing my shoulders and the back of my neck.

"Is something out there?" she continued.

"Well, you wouldn't believe me if I told you, so I won't."

Sliding back over to the kitchen, she handed me a vase that she had rustled out of the cupboard and said, "Here, see if we can resurrect that poor little plant. It may take two to three days to see if it will come back to life if at all."

I hadn't moved. I was still standing frozen in place, staring out into the garden.

"Come on now, dear; tell me what's bothering you."

"Okay, I will, but don't worry about it. I am sure it was just the glint off the window or something, but I swear I saw that purple gladiola, well …" I hesitated. "She winked at me."

I glanced at my wife to see how she was going to react to such a crazy assertion. Without moving her head, her eyes shifted back to me, the gladiolas, and then back to me.

I cut into the eerie silence. "Hmm. Must be that I am not fully awake yet. Not to worry." Shaking my empty hand in the air to dismiss the illusion, I headed to the sink to fill the vase with water and gently placed the rose of Sharon inside, with hopes that it would resurrect itself and regain the beauty it had displayed in the backyard as it tried to bring peace to the garden of discontent.

> *"Not that I speak in respect of want: for I have learned, in whatsoever state I am, [therewith] to be content. I know how to get along with humble means, and I also know how to live in prosperity; in any and every circumstance I have learned the secret of being filled and going hungry, both of having abundance and suffering need."*
>
> Philippians 4:11–12 (KJV)

Marinating Moments

Notice that Paul writes that he has "learned" to be content. Contentment, *true* contentment, apparently is a learned or a learning process in our walk with God.

1. What does contentment look like to you?
2. What sort of curriculum would you put together for students to "learn" to be content?
3. What materials do we have to study to learn contentment?
4. Which plant in the story do you most closely relate to?

Marinade 4:

Can We Be Content ... Really?

"For I have learned, in whatsoever state I am, to be content."

Philippians 4:11b (NKJV)

As Americans, we have the blessed opportunity to live the dream life, which typically constitutes a wealth of material *things*, like cars, homes, and a carefree stroll through the mall. Merrily, merrily, life is but a dream.

However, in this merry life of ours, are we as content as God wants us to be? Answering that may take a little soul-searching and a reality check.

Webster's definition of *contentment* is "Happy enough with what one has or is, not desiring something more or different. Satisfied. Also; to satisfy the mind so as to stop complaint."

To *stop* complaint? What Earth is Webster from?

The problem begins with becoming weary of the words that express our societal problems. Words that seem to drag us down are *AIG, stimulus, trillions, national debt,* etc. All-important words in this critical time, to be sure; however, I think they are disturbing my *contentment*. In this state of national financial stress and insecurity, how is your contentment holding out?

Perhaps a reality check requires the use of relativism. Allow me to introduce you to Pappy. He's a hardworking man, putting six to seven days a week into his own business on the corner of 7th Ave and Lincoln. I mean, literally on the corner. He starts at 4 a.m. on weekdays but sleeps in till 5 a.m. on weekends, don't you know. "Gotta catch the coffee crowd," he claims. Every day he grabs his own cup of coffee, a three-ring binder, his Salvation Army bag filled with goodies, a stepstool to sit on, his cigarettes, and he heads to work. His three-ring binder is an important trade tool for his job, because inside the protective plastic sleeve, he hangs out his business sign which says: "Good Morning, Have a great Day. One Love, Anything helps." Once the sign is up, the business begins. (With a cross separating the words "One" and "Love.")

Pappy has no need for a car. Besides, not having a driver's license doesn't get in the way if you walk to work every day. Anyway, since he has spent nine and a half years in the Oklahoma State Penitentiary, getting licenses of any kind becomes a chore.

> ### "I AM DEVOTED TO THE CREATOR WHO TAKES CARE OF ME ON THIS CORNER."

"I am devoted to the Creator who takes care of me on this corner," states Pappy as he flashes a V for peace to everyone who passes by. "Yeah, Love," he continues as he looks at me and then at traffic like an avid angler watching for a nibble. "Love is greater than the commandments. His love has sustained me these past fifteen months on this corner."

Originally from Woodward, Oklahoma, Pappy eventually landed in Eugene. He loves it here. He claims that, "Eugene has its own unique perspective of other people's spiritual opinions." Huh?

He shared a bit of his own testimony. "I felt Christ come into me when I was twelve years old. Then I was baptized in a pond. I always want to listen to that still small voice in my heart."

I asked him if he was happy, or even content, in this state of his life. "Happy?" he asked as he grabbed a bill from a passing motorist.

"I am more than happy! They call me Happy Pappy sometimes too." Flashing a V sign to passing cars. "As the Lord leads, people give."

Once, a flashy red, monstrous truck whisks by, and the driver tosses a wadded-up bill at Pappy. With it comes an apology. "Sorry to throw it at you, but the light is green, gotta keep moving!" yells the driver as he zooms past.

I marveled at Pappy's vocabulary, which reflected a depth of education. "Oh, that's because my dad used to lock up my brother and me in a room and made us memorize 'Word Power' from *Reader's Digest*. We got pretty good at it too." He flashed a huge, toothless grin that was framed by his nicotine-stained mustache and beard. Yet, despite the distraction that the matted beard and disheveled hair caused me, I could definitely discern the twinkling sparkle in his eyes.

As I looked around at his little portable office setting, he saw that I noticed a pack of his cigarettes. Immediately his face flushed, and he apologetically said, "Some things I can't kick! I drink a little too." Looking at traffic he tossed back over his shoulder, "For medicinal purposes only though!"

A couple honks and cheers went up as the regulars called his name. "Hey Pappy, how's the day?" they would yell out as they passed by. While accepting a handout, he would always reply, "May your blessings be returned to you a thousandfold."

"Oh," he added, as if he wasn't done explaining the cigarettes, "I smoke a little marijuana from time to time. For medicinal purposes only though."

"Do you have any words for the church?" I asked.

"Yeah," he replied, without hesitation and with an intense gaze. "Brothers, sisters, live in your faith, not in your works. Love God and your neighbors!" Good word, Pappy.

It was obvious that life had not been kind to

> WHILE ACCEPTING A HANDOUT, HE WOULD ALWAYS REPLY, "MAY YOUR BLESSINGS BE RETURNED TO YOU A THOUSANDFOLD."

him over the years. I placed him in his seventies; actually, he had just turned sixty. He faults "too many drugs, alcohol, and plastic women."

When his shift is over, he will head over to the Food for Lane County kitchen to eat. Then to his motel room on 7th Ave for the night. Nevertheless, it was a joy to watch him ply his trade. Whether working the crowd or his regulars, you couldn't help but sense his contentment. His attitude, his demeanor, but mostly his peace made me think of Hebrews 13:2—"Be not forgetful to receive strangers; for thereby some have entertained angels without realizing it."

We know the old saw that's been drummed into our heads which states that it's not wrong to *have* nice things. Moreover, it's not wrong to take *care* of them; the Bible even encourages us to do so. The differentiation is in our hearts and minds regarding the drive and motivation and the priority we exhibit to even *want* them. Our treasure is where our heart is … are we *content* with what we have? Satisfied, without complaint?

As I left Pappy, I decided to drive around the block and approach him in my car. He recognized me and flashed a grin. I handed him a bill, and he recited his mantra, only slightly modified: "May your blessing be returned to you *ten* thousandfold!" With a quick "Amen, Brother," the light changed and I headed up the bridge. In my rearview mirror I caught a glimpse of his V and that charming toothless grin that spoke of his "gain through contentment."

"But Godliness, with contentment, is great gain."

1 Timothy 6:6 (KJV)

"But I have calmed and quieted myself, I am like a weaned child with its mother; like a weaned child I am content."

Psalm 131:2

"The fear of the Lord leads to life; then one rests content, untouched by trouble."

Proverbs 19:23

Marinating Moments

1. It is obvious, as Scripture states, that the "state of contentment" is a learned attribute—not necessarily something you are born with. Share what you do to learn to be content.

2. In the story, it appears that Pappy attempts to give something back. His attitude, a smile, the twinkle of his eye, even hope! How well are you doing at transmitting those attitudes?

3. Do you have friends or acquaintances like Pappy? Do you pray for your friends to get their lives straightened out? If they have Christ, is that enough?

4. What could or should you do to change your attitude to that of being content?

Marinade 5:

From the Crèche to the Cross:
A Mother's Memories

"Carrying his own cross, he went out to the place of the Skull (which in Aramaic is called Golgotha)."

John 19:17

It was nearing the ninth hour, about high noon. Inexplicably, the sky had been darkening for the past three hours; the earth had been convulsing uncontrollably, and the people of Jerusalem were scurrying about in wild alarm, trying to make sense of the phenomena they were experiencing.

Whispers among the scrambling throngs consistently focused on the events of the day. *"Hey, did you hear what happened in the temple, in the Holy of Holies? I hear that the veil has been torn; yeah, can you believe it? Actually ripped in half, from the top to the bottom—and nobody knows who did it! I hear that the temple guards are searching for the culprit right now. Amazing stuff,*

"Carrying his own cross, he went out to the place of the Skull (which in Aramaic is called Golgotha)."

John 19:17

> **WOULD TRUTH BE THE HEINOUS CRIME THAT SENTENCED HIM TO DEATH? YOU CAN KILL THE MAN, BUT YOU CAN'T KILL THE TRUTH.**

huh?" Whisper, whisper, whisper …

At the center of this bustling confusion were three occupied crosses, silhouetted against the darkening skies … three crosses … with three men suspended by their limbs, two of whom had been convicted of crimes committed against their fellow man. The one in the middle, sources said, hadn't done anything worthy of the punishment he was receiving.

Okay, so they said that the one in the middle made claims. Claims that made him guilty of blasphemy; claims that got him killed. He claimed that He was sent by God—but what if He was! They said He claimed that He was the Son of God—but what if He was! They also said that He claimed that He was God—well, what if He was! What if He was all three of those things? Would truth be the heinous crime that sentenced Him to death? You can kill the man, but you can't kill the truth.

Even Pontius Pilate eventually didn't want to have anything to do with His case. In his famous oratory at the man's sentencing, Pilate had asserted as much: "I wash my hands of this innocent man's blood!" he had declared.

Overshadowed by the looming cross was a lone, stoic figure, like an immovabe sentry stationed directly beneath it. The figure gently swiped at the tears that streamed down her cheeks as she slumped to her knees at the foot of the pillory. One tear after another cascaded down her face until the parched well could not summon one drop more. With swollen eyes and drained tear ducts the lone woman, Mary, the mother of Jesus, stood watch at the foot of the cross … the cross in the middle.

Frozen in place by grief, she looked upon her son as He agonizingly hung in His preassigned position. Not assigned by a Roman procurator. Not assigned by zealous religious rulers, but preassigned by sin, before the earth was even formed. His mission, to hang on a tree, was issued before that tree had ever taken root. Before the seed of the tree had even been formed. Before the soil for the seed to penetrate had been created. Before the atmosphere had developed to nurture a continent to plant a seed to grow a tree for Him to die on. Even before a universe was formed to create a planet that would nurture that continent. But why this specifically gory assignment? The simple, yet supernaturally fed answer is: for the salvation of mankind before mankind existed. Demonstrating forward thinking to the nth degree on God's part.

Mary longingly gazed at His arms, stained by the dark red blood that had oozed from his pinned-down hands ... those same little arms that used to help his daddy carry wood and swing a hammer are pinned to the wood that are carrying His arms now. "Yehoshua, the carpenter's son"—that's how the neighbors knew him. He worked side by side with his earthly dad for years learning the trade, though not really intending to make it a career. He always knew he had a different woodworking call.

Mom stared at those blood-streaked arms, recalling the times when those same tiny arms would wrap around her neck as she prayed for God to bless His sleep.

> MOM STARED AT THOSE BLOOD-STREAKED ARMS, RECALLING THE TIMES WHEN THOSE SAME TINY ARMS WOULD WRAP AROUND HER NECK AS SHE PRAYED FOR GOD TO BLESS HIS SLEEP.

The arms that only last week healed the sick and brought strength to the lame now hung in a motionless, outstretched position, demonstrating to all of mankind just how infinitely far His love for humanity would extend. Oh, how Mom wanted to run up to Him, hold His head in her arms, soothe His aching muscles, and dab away the dried blood from the wound in His side!

She looked at His legs that were pegged to the splintery cross by a jagged metal spike—not a simple nail, but a spike that was wedged into his feet, splitting the tender bones and straining the ligaments, resulting in excruciating pain. To her, those were the same happy little feet that once carried a boyish Yehoshua from the house out to the playground. The same feet that once walked the dusty highways and byways of the Promised Land, teaching and introducing fragile men and women to the magnificent God of grace, all the while teaching about the love and the wonders of God Himself.

It's at a time like this that a mother's memories overwhelmingly flood back into the forefront of her grief-stricken mind ... memories that serve to endear and bond her to her child. Snapshot after snapshot, times of yesteryear flashed by as Mary reviewed the years of His life—just over thirty-two in all. She smiled to herself as she thought back ... back to the very beginning and the fond memories of that day when Joseph was on bended knee and she replied "Yes" as he asked for her hand in marriage. She still remembered the fear she had knowing he was going to ask her father the same question!

Slowly the images in her head passed in review as she recalled that night in her room when an angel of the Lord hailed her as "highly favored among women." For centuries Hebrew women had longed to be the chosen one to bear the promised Messiah, praying that they might be selected to be honored by God. Remembering the sheer terror that had filled her heart that night caused her to shudder. Wouldn't you feel the same if suddenly your room was awash in the glow of a brilliant, white, shining light, and a stranger claiming to be an angel by the name of Gabriel were addressing you?

Glancing down at her abdomen, she recalled the adrenaline that had filled her body as she knew that conception had occurred: a special child, a holy child was being formed in her womb! The thrill, the excitement, the overwhelming joy that coursed through her very being as she knew that God had touched her as he had never touched another woman! But then fear returned, and Mary's spirits had plummeted as she thought, *How am I going to tell Joseph?*

What relief poured over her when Joseph disclosed to her that an angel had told him that it was God who had done this and that no shame would come upon her head. Finally, the long-awaited Messiah was in-utero, and Mary was the chosen one. Centuries of generations had gone by; millions of women had dreamt it would be them ...

but Mary of Nazareth was to be the favored among women, and the Messiah was to be born!

The pregnancy had not been one of the more delightful times of her life, except for her visits to Elizabeth. How she had been welcomed! She recalled that arduous journey from Nazareth to Bethlehem—seventy miles (on donkey back no less), and just at her time of delivery, to be counted for the census. That was about all she could endure. Arriving in Bethlehem and longing for a good night's sleep on a comfy mattress and a place to wash up after a dusty, bumpy voyage, all that expectation—only to be met with disappointment and rejection.

There was no room for them anywhere in town, except, well . . . there was this one place, though they'd have to share it. When they got there, it was occupied all right, but the occupants were the animals that God intended to be witnesses to the birth of all births: the birth of the King of all Kings. God was coming to pay them a stable call!

Baby Jesus entered the world like any other child: labor pains, heavy breathing, and dear ol' Dad at Mary's side with words of comfort to ease her through the pain and ordeal of childbirth. Joseph was reassuring, reminding her of what the angel had prophesied:

CENTURIES OF GENERATIONS HAD GONE BY; MILLIONS OF WOMEN HAD DREAMT IT WOULD BE THEM . . . BUT MARY OF NAZARETH WAS TO BE THE FAVORED AMONG WOMEN, AND THE MESSIAH WAS TO BE BORN!

BABY JESUS ENTERED THE WORLD LIKE ANY OTHER CHILD: LABOR PAINS, HEAVY BREATHING, AND DEAR OL' DAD AT MARY'S SIDE WITH WORDS OF COMFORT TO EASE HER THROUGH THE PAIN AND ORDEAL OF CHILDBIRTH.

that she was indeed blessed among women. Any father knows that the selection of words to a woman in labor, especially during the most painful and irritable stage of birth called transition, have to be well thought-out and well presented. Joseph was safe. He merely reminded her of God's overall plan, and that she was right in the middle of it.

Soon afterward, as with most mothers, the pain of childbirth was overtaken by the joys of motherhood. The sight of her swaddled baby boy, lying in a manger, served to anesthetize Mary from any lingering pain associated with the birth of this special child. They named the baby Yehoshua. In Greek it is translated Jesus.

Outside the stable there was a great commotion in the streets of Bethlehem. People were scurrying about, visibly put off by the approaching shepherds who were running and shouting so stridently, disturbing the townsfolk. Traditionally, shepherds were required to stay outside the city limits, yet these shepherds were so electrified they couldn't help but violate the custom. What they had seen, what they had heard, what they had experienced that night could not be restrained by tradition or convention.

Running through the little town of Bethlehem, they were telling everyone about the early morning visitation by the host of angels as they were watching their sheep. Out of nowhere, an angel had appeared to them and announced the birth of the Messiah in Bethlehem! Then all of a sudden, not just one angel but a whole host appeared and started singing—a truly angelic choir, no sour notes, no one off key. A beautiful rendition of the original "O Little Town of Bethlehem" rang out across the verdant hills.

Jumping from person to person, the shepherds' joy and excitement began to spread, stirring the townsfolk. "The Messiah has come!" was being shouted from house to house.

As she continued to scan through her mental photo album, Mary remembered her joy when Joseph came to her one day and told her that he'd found a house for their new little family to live in. One day, a knock came at the door of that house … a visitation that she would never forget. Opening the door, Mary's eyes fell upon the stately figures of men clothed in magnificent vestments—obviously royalty from eastern kingdoms. Having learned through the Jewish Scriptures that a king was to be born, and following the path lit by an immovable, brilliant star, hung like a spotlight in the heavens by God Himself, they had set their course for Israel to pay homage to the baby king.

These men from the East came not only with gifts to adorn the new king, but also with a wise warning: "Herod is upset, and he's looking for Jesus too ... not to adorn Him with fine gifts either." King Herod had no regard for life—especially that of a little child. In his pursuit of Jesus, he lived up to his evil reputation by having every little two-year-old baby boy in the region put to death. When the emperor, Caesar Augustus, heard of Herod's decree to have the children murdered, he coined a phrase: "It is better to have been one of Herod's pigs than one of his children."

The wise men's warning required yet another donkey ride for the young family—this time a life-saving flight to Egypt.

The gentle touch of John wrapping his arms around Mary's shoulders jolted her back to the present—back to the scene of the crime. The crime . . . what crime? Was the crime God living among man, or man hanging God on a tree? Whose fault was that? The Romans—because it was their way of dealing with capital crimes? Or the Jews—because they didn't recognize that they had God in their presence? Their long awaited Messiah had arrived, right on schedule, but they couldn't see it. They didn't want to see it.

> THE GENTLE TOUCH OF JOHN WRAPPING HIS ARMS AROUND MARY'S SHOULDERS JOLTED HER BACK TO THE PRESENT—BACK TO THE SCENE OF THE CRIME. THE CRIME ... WHAT CRIME? WAS THE CRIME GOD LIVING AMONG MAN, OR MAN HANGING GOD ON A TREE?

Despite the lightning bolts of searing pain that crackled throughout his wracked body, at time when every raw nerve ending throughout His body was dialing 911 for help, Jesus looked out at those people standing there. Some were jeering, some were crying, confusion abounded, yet He asked His Father in heaven to forgive them, because they really didn't realize what they were doing. Therefore, it can be concluded that neither Roman nor Jew were at fault: this scene had to occur, because Roman and Hebrew, Gentile and Jew were at fault collectively—it was all their fault (and ours) before a faultless God that required this scene to unfold.

Mary and John, standing together at the foot of the cross . . . neither had any more tears to squeeze out of their gritty eyes. Both realized that they found themselves alone at the foot of the cross. Most of the disciples had fled for fear of being accused of associating with this Jesus, the King of the Jews. But Mary, faithful Mary—Mom— never left His side. That was her son hanging there. How could she possibly abandon him here, and at this critical time?

Jesus's central nervous system was becoming overloaded, shorting out signals from the muscles to the brain. Jolts fired through a network of flared nerves. Swollen hands and feet searing with crackling pulses transmitted messages to his brain, tapping out SOS's for help, but none was on the way. No more physical data could be accepted as his whipped bare, raw, and welted back scraped against the jagged, splintery wood of the cross. In one final gesture, Jesus garnered just enough strength to speak, and in unbearable agony He looked favorably upon His mother and commended her into the care and safekeeping of His dearest disciple, John.

Soon, the final, tender, and historical words

SOON, THE FINAL, TENDER, AND HISTORICAL WORDS "TE TELESTAI" ("IT IS FINISHED") CAME THROUGH THE PARCHED LIPS OF JESUS AND ROLLED OUT INTO ETERNITY. THOSE WERE AMONG HER SON'S FINAL WORDS.

"te telestai" ("it is finished") came through the parched lips of Jesus and rolled out into eternity. Those were among her son's final words.

Mary was awesome through all this. Awesome in her faith and in her faithfulness. Mothers have a way of seeing something different in their children—something that others, even fathers, don't see. It's a mysterious, uncanny, natural ability that God has implanted into women that gives them a certain edge in parenting. As difficult as it was to watch this event take place, Mary had a certain peace about her. She knew the prophecies about the Messiah. She knew that Daniel, the prophet, wrote that after the Messiah was revealed, He was to be cut off by His own people before He took power (Daniel 9:25–27). She also believed that if He was truly the Son of God, as had been testified to her, then surely, some way, somehow, He would rise again!

It was only three days that Mary was without Jesus. In the wee hours of the morning of the third day, as if pulled by an unseen hand of prophetic knowledge, Mary and her friend Mary Magdalene arose early and started for the tomb where their friends had laid Jesus. Trying with all their might to believe, they recited the Scriptures that promised a risen Savior. Despite the nagging thoughts of doubt, they reassured each other that a mere tomb could not hold Jesus. Suddenly, they felt the ground begin to shake. There was no doubt about that feeling … earthquake!

In the midst of the wrenching sounds of a convulsing earth, Mary was awestruck as they neared the tomb and she saw a familiar, brilliant light begin to glow. She'd seen that glow before! The telltale glow that heralds the appearance of an angel, one who had been assigned "tour guide" duty to demonstrate that the tomb was indeed empty! Jesus had in fact risen from the dead, just as He said He would.

Mary no longer stands alone at the foot of the cross. Now, she is accompanied by many a believer who has chosen to follow a risen Jesus.

Centuries have elapsed since that turn of events. Man in all his folly has spent hours upon hours trying to explain away the phenomenon of Jesus, the Christ of Nazareth.

Theory after theory has punctuated the minds of many ... but none have been able to—nor ever will—explain away the fact that the tomb was empty.

Empty!

And it remains that way to this day! A short tour of the garden tomb in Jerusalem today will confirm it!

Jesus kept His promise ... He said, "On the third Day I will rise again," and so He did!

The tomb is empty because Jesus conquered human death, and even now He is alive. We can have a real relationship with Him because He lived as we live, and He knows our sorrows, our trials and hurts. Jesus knew the drill before He left heaven; He had to experience pain, sorrow, grief, confusion, and other human sufferings so that when we call out to Him in our pain, He can say, "I understand." Scripture tells us that this same Jesus now sits at the right hand of the Father, forever interceding on our behalf.

Mary was blessed because she was there: she saw and believed. Jesus says that *we* are even more blessed. Based on the fact that we *weren't* there, we didn't see, or hear, or experience Him personally, and yet we believe. Jesus Himself says, "Because you have seen me, you have believed; blessed are those who have not seen and yet have believed" (John 20:29).

D. Elton Trueblood wrote, "Faith is not belief without proof, but trust without reservation."

It is this Jesus, Mary's little boy, the promised Messiah, the Son of God, whose birthday we celebrate at Christmas, a special time of year. A time to celebrate the advent of a special child: God's.

And it is His death and resurrection that we commemorate at Eastertime.

But it is this Jesus, the Christ, whose birthday

> SCRIPTURE TELLS US THAT THIS SAME JESUS NOW SITS AT THE RIGHT HAND OF THE FATHER, FOREVER INTERCEDING ON OUR BEHALF.

wouldn't be worth celebrating if He hadn't done what He said He would do on the cross. A Jesus who, as the words of the hymn state, "Now talks with us and walks with us, along life's narrow way." A risen Savior who offers us a personal relationship with Himself. Does that sound like religion to you, or pure grace?

> *"For to us a child is born, to us a son is given, and the government will be on his shoulders. And he will be called Wonderful Counselor, Mighty God, Everlasting Father, Prince of Peace."*
>
> Isaiah 9:6

Marinating Moments

1. Jesus was crucified for telling the truth. When truth enters your life, how do you receive it? What if you don't want to hear it?

2. Jesus identified deeply with human life and suffering. Where has He met you in your suffering? How might you take your suffering to Him?

3. Mary saw something in Jesus that no one else did that allowed her to stay faithful through the darkest time. What do you think she saw in Him that so strengthened her faith?

Marinade 6:

A Mother's Memories: Postscript

*"For I resolved to know nothing while I was with you except
Jesus Christ and him crucified."*

1 Corinthians 2:2

Originally, the word *holiday* was two separate words: *holy day*. Most
of our holidays remain "holy days," but they have been marred by
commercialism.

Which brings up a vital family issue: What have you taught your
children about the holy days of Christmas and Easter? We have just
spent time reviewing the birth and death of Jesus, the Christ, and the
powerful message of salvation they send. But our discussion leaves room
to repeat: when that time of year rolls around, that time we call the holidays, what is the excitement in your life and family centered around?

Is it about Santa Claus? The omnipresent jolly old fat guy who
sees you when you're sleeping? The bearded old man who knows if
you're naughty or nice? Is that what your children think is the reason
for the Christmas celebration?

I'll never forget the ringing in my ears when I received a call from
a family member who was complaining to me that my own three-
year-old son had "ruined Christmas" for her son, his cousin, because
he dared to tell him the truth ... my son flat-out said that Santa Claus
wasn't real and Jesus was the reason for the season!

That three-year-old boy mustered more guts than most adults. He dared to break through the barrier of delusion that has been thrown up to mask the real reason for the Christmas season.

Today's mantra is "Let's take Christ out of *CHRIST*mas; because it's religion!"

"What's He doing there anyway?" the world asks. "Why, this is the time of cheer and goodwill toward men, a time when man extends his hand of peace and lowers his weapons of warfare. Your religion doesn't belong in the middle of it!"

Really? Jesus is *all about* peace and goodwill toward men!

The devil himself, digging deep into his bag of foils, says, "How can I get them to take their attention away from the cross of the Christ? And the empty tomb of Christ? Hmm, I know what I can do. I'll get man to dream up some imaginary beneficent old guy who lives with his wife in the North Pole and has a bunch of elves making toys year-round, so that on one preselected night a year—oh, let's use Christmas—he'll hitch up flying reindeer, load enough toys to supply an entire world full of kids, and tell his wife to have dinner ready when he returns. He'll take off on a flight that even if he traveled at the speed of light he couldn't accomplish in one night ..."

Couldn't you just picture the devil saying, as he sinisterly twirls the tips of his moustache, "Yeah, that'll work, man will fall for that ... they'll go for it. They'll buy into the lie that Jesus is just a fairy tale and Santa Claus is gospel! If I work on it a bit, I'll bet they'll even go for rabbits laying colored eggs, and they'll convince their children too."

Look, I am not trying to ruin the holiday for you, or traditions that you've come to love and enjoy. I *do* want to make them more special for you by keeping the focus on Jesus.

If you are still telling your kids about Santa Claus and the Easter Bunny, then it's time to come clean. Tell them about Jesus Christ! Men, if your wife is still telling you that Santa brought you something because she doesn't want to ruin your Christmas ... then you better grow up!

Teaching your kids that Jesus is the reason for the season really won't ruin their Christmas. It will enhance their Christmas and make the time of giving more special. Additionally, you won't have to leave cookies and milk out

> IF YOU ARE STILL TELLING YOUR KIDS ABOUT SANTA CLAUS AND THE EASTER BUNNY, THEN IT'S TIME TO COME CLEAN. TELL THEM ABOUT JESUS CHRIST!

anymore (and then eat them yourselves and tell the kids that Santa ate them. My parents did that). You won't have to feel guilty because their little broken hearts were crushed when Santa didn't leave them the shiny bike they were hoping for and they got underwear instead (my parents did that too)!

The bottom line: resist the cultural substitution of Santa Claus for Christ at Christmas.

I am not trying to ruin ages-old tradition! However, I am encour-

> THE BOTTOM LINE: RESIST THE CULTURAL SUBSTITUTION OF SANTA CLAUS FOR CHRIST AT CHRISTMAS.

aging you to rejoice in a risen Savior, whose birth we celebrate on Christmas Day, who also died and rose again from the dead. Why? So that today you don't have to wallow in the consequences of your sins any longer.

God became a man to be the propitiation for *our* sins. *Propitiation* is a two-dollar word that means *advocate*. Jesus, the Christ, has become our advocate. Through Christ we are reconciled to God, who sees us as sinless as a result of placing our trust and faith in Him.

Mary stands at the foot of the cross in the pain of the moment. We, too, can stand at the foot of the cross—but in the joy of the moment.

What's your choice?

"I have been crucified with Christ and I no longer live,
but Christ lives in me. The life I now live in the body, I live
by faith in the Son of God, who loved me and gave
himself for me."

Galatians 2:20

Marinating Moments

1. How do you handle the holidays? What traditions and beliefs are important to you as a family?

2. Have you ever seen the connection of Christmas and Easter as literally "holy days"? How can you honor the holiness of these days in practical or internal ways?

3. Do you think it's a problem to teach your children that Santa Claus exists? Why or why not? What problems do you think these myths might be causing in our society, if any?

4. Write down one specific way you will commit to turn your attention to the holiness of Christ this Christmas or Easter season.

Marinade 7:

That Fellow from Nazareth

"Go away! What do you want with us, Jesus of Nazareth? Have you come to destroy us? I know who you are—the Holy One of God!"

Luke 4:34

From the east, the terminator line that separates the darkness of night from the light of day was galloping westward across the Judean desert, chasing the sun into the sea. Along the way, it swallowed every last photon of light as it swooped down through the Dead Sea valley, over the top of the former Soddom and Gomorrah, then enshrouded the Masada plateau. Now, it was scaling the escarpment of the Judean foothills and bearing down on what is known as Mount Moriah.

In the west, the retreating sun appeared like a coin in a slot, seemingly wedged between two mountain peaks. Only fading shafts of reddish-orange light were visible as it began to nestle into the western sky, preparing to be tucked in for the night. The receedng sun issued final slivers of light that splashed iridescent reds and pinks off the lingering canvas of the high cirrus clouds. One by one, pinpoints of white starlight began to gradually pierce through the final vestiges of the purple veil that hovered over the Judean skies.

> CANDLES WERE BEING LIT, BEDS WERE BEING TURNED DOWN, TEETH WERE BEING BRUSHED, TRASHCAN LIDS WERE BEING SLAMMED SHUT, AND DOGS WERE BAYING AT THE MOON AS IT STRADDLED THE CONFLU-ENCE OF DAY AND DARK.

In between the approaching night and the setting sun, it was twilight over Jerusalem. The night air was filled with the sounds of clanking dinner dishes being placed in drain boards, sounds that were matched only by giggling children as they slipped into their pajamas.

Candles were being lit, beds were being turned down, teeth were being brushed, trashcan lids were being slammed shut, and dogs were baying at the moon as it straddled the confluence of day and dark. All this activity was in preparation for the coming night. Peace, and her cousin Tranquility, hung over the city, waiting to settle over the slumbering citizens.

All is right in Jerusalem, except with you.

So shaken are you about the events that have transpired in Jerusalem this day that you've decided that you have to take a walk. Perhaps, you think, a little fresh air will do you a world of good. A leg-stretching stroll along a garden path will help shake the pervasive thoughts from your mind of the crazy events that have taken place on the temple mount.

Before long you find yourself in one of your favorite garden spots in all of Jerusalem, or even all of Israel for that matter. Wandering aimlessly along the path, only stopping from time to time to sniff a flower or toss a couple of pebbles around, you are entranced in thought, even mired in confusion. Thoughts swirl in your head like a tornado. If you don't settle them soon, you fear that you'll have "scrambled brain syndrome." The things that so rocked Jerusalem this morning continue to shake you this evening.

This new guy named Yeshua, Jesus to some, that fellow from Nazareth, has consumed your thoughts and intrigued the entire city.

The funny thing is that you are bouncing back and forth from the humorous, chuckling as you think of Nazarenes—what good thing has ever come from the Galilee region?—to the serious, pondering this striking young evangelist who has gathered a following of zealous believers in such a short amount of time. Some say that He has only been teaching His message now for about three years. Yet something is arresting about the young man, despite the fact that gathering a flock of followers isn't all that unusual; people follow after folks with new ideas all the time. No, with this charismatic preacher from Galilee, it's something different. You are stumped at the logic that He speaks with and the amazing knowledge He has of Scripture. Especially of the prophets. The special prophets, the anointed prophets, the prophets who wrote of the coming Messiah. Yeshua knows them well. He knows them exceptionally well.

Yes, many false Messiahs have walked the dusty paths of Judea, but to you, there is a different feeling about this guy. Especially of interest is the rumor circulating from a wedding over in Cana, right next door to Nazareth. You wonder if there really is any validity to the incident you heard about. Surely, you aren't going to fall for the gossipers and their fanciful tales of water-to-wine hoaxes, and the rumors circulating around the gossip circles about His mother really being a virgin! How could that be? Once again chuckles seep out between your lips.

However, reality grips you again as the incident at the temple continues to bother you the most. Tossing a twig that you've twisted into a pretzel, you almost feel like blurting out, "Who does this guy think He is, making a whip and rousting all the merchandisers from the temple area . . . how else were people supposed to purchase their sacrifices and present themselves to the priest?" Heaving a huge sigh, you shake a piece of gravel from your sandal, pivot in the middle of the path, and begin to head for home.

> HOWEVER, REALITY GRIPS YOU AGAIN AS THE INCIDENT AT THE TEMPLE CONTINUES TO BOTHER YOU THE MOST.

Just as soon as you are ready to quit thinking about it and turn your thoughts to Passover, you overhear voices on the other side of a hedgerow. The man's voice just a couple of shrubs away sounds very familiar. He apparently hasn't seen or heard you. Curious, you extend your arms to clear away some of the bushes that will allow you to peek through. That's when you recognize him. It's Rabbi Nicodemus!

And then you gasp! The other voice is that fellow from Nazareth. Nicodemous is talking with that Yeshua guy—in private!

Perhaps the two men think there is nobody within eyesight or even earshot, because what Nicodemus is about to do would put him at great risk with the Sanhedrin. Specifically, the Pharisee Division. Anybody who is going to come in and disturb their established hierarchy of VIPs (Very Important Pharisees . . . actually, it's more like Very Introuble Pilferers!) will certainly not be welcomed.

You are about to overhear perhaps the most important conversation in all the land. History will note it as perhaps the most important conversation in the entire Bible.

> YOU ARE ABOUT TO OVERHEAR PERHAPS THE MOST IMPORTANT CONVERSATION IN ALL THE LAND. HISTORY WILL NOTE IT AS PERHAPS THE MOST IMPORTANT CONVERSATION IN THE ENTIRE BIBLE.

You can't believe what you are hearing in the garden. Nicodemus, a man you highly respect, speaking with this rabbi—this rabble-rouser fellow. This table-turner and temple upsetter. And Nicodemous is actually listening. You pull your arms back, half with the thought of covering your mouth to prevent any audible gasping sounds from escaping, and half with a sense of dismay. How can you ever trust Nicodemous again—especially after he has been contaminated by this man's twisted religious ideas?

Leaning forward into the bush and brushing aside just enough of the leaves to get a view of the two men seated on a garden bench, you strain to listen, feeling half-bad that you are eavesdropping but also worried about your Chief Rabbi Nicodemous. That's when something catches your ears, spoken by this Jesus fellow, that perks you up and riles your insides:

". . . that whosoever believeth in me . . . should not perish, but have eternal life."

Instantly you become offended and almost blow your cover behind the bush. *Hey!* you shout to yourself. *That's Messiah talk! Who does He think He is anyway!* Once again you rock back on your heels, trying to make sense of what you're hearing.

Without any effort on your part, you can hear the conversation through the bush. Then He floors you with this: "For God so loves the world, that He has sent *me*, His only son, to die as a sacrificial lamb for the sins of that world that He so loves."

> "FOR GOD SO LOVES THE WORLD, THAT HE HAS SENT *ME*, HIS ONLY SON, TO DIE AS A SACRIFICIAL LAMB FOR THE SINS OF THAT WORLD THAT HE SO LOVES."

Now, there's some food for your thoughts: "God so loved the world … that . . ."

"That" what? The word *that* is a powerful connective word!

Jesus is implying that God's love for man existed before man existed! What *you* hear is that His love, for you, is not even conditional upon your existence. You weren't even a gleam in your parents' eyes, and He loved you . . . and that was even before your parents were around. Now you're bombarded by a billion thoughts. There has to be a way to catch this rabble-rouser at his own game. And you come up with it! *Aha,* you think brilliantly. *I haven't heard Him place conditions yet. Surely there will be conditions. Like, if you follow my commandments, I will love you!* Hmm, but He doesn't seem to say that.

You think up other conditions that He'll surely impose. Let's see if He says something like, "If you do the things that I require of you, *then* I will love you." If that doesn't work, how about this as a condition: "If you believe in God, *then* I will love you." Or one more thought flashes through your mind: "If you pedal your bicycle from door to door and evangelize, *then* I will love you."

Where are the dos and the don'ts? Where are the performance evaluation forms?

(Let's face it, as readers, we know that God's love for us is unconditional. And we know that our salvation rests only on one work of ours, and that work is this: What have we done about Jesus the Christ? The Son who was sent into the world that it might not be condemned by Him, but saved by Him.)

Behind the safety of the bush, your mind continues to process and whir like a computer, and you start to discount His story by trying to remember the Torah and the characters that God dealt with there ... down deep you're determined to disprove this guy, and to prove that God actually works on a conditonal basis.

Now, hmm, there was Moses. Surely his antics caused him trouble with God. You remember that in Exodus chapter 2, Moses killed an Egyptian guard. Surely God's favor on Moses was limited because of that act of the flesh!

Then you recall in Numbers chapter 20, where Moses was told to smite the rock once to get water from it! But out of anger, he struck it twice! Surely God's love for him waned at that point.

Yet you recall Deuteronomy 34:10-12:

> Since then, no prophet has risen in Israel like Moses, whom the Lord knew face to face, who did all those signs and wonders the Lord sent him to do in Egypt—to Pharaoh and to all his officials and to his whole land. For no one has ever shown the mighty power or performed the awesome deeds that Moses did in the sight of all Israel.

All right, so that didn't work; God used Moses mightily, even through Moses's human failures and weaknesses. So you jump to

Elijah: now there's a fellow who surely was forsaken by God! After killing the prophets of Baal, and basking in that mighty victory on Mount Carmel, he gets a notice from Queen Jezebel in 1 Kings 19:3: "Dear Mr. Elijah, you have murdered my people; now I promise to make you dead like they are within 24 hrs" (author's version).

You recall that in verse 3 it says, "and when he saw that, he arose and fled for his life." Aha! You're sure that God wouldn't tolerate that kind of lack of faith, right on the heels of such a great victory … no way!

But as you think about it, you realize (doh!) that God not only continues to love Elijah, He even tends to his physical needs and comes quietly to him and assigns him more jobs to do. Later on, in 2 Kings 2:11, you remember that God even sends a chauffeur in a flaming chariot to come escort Elijah home to heaven.

Rats, that didn't help prove your point either.

Nope, you are hard-pressed to find any character in the Bible whom God didn't love without conditions attached.

Wait a minute, how about Jezebel herself?

(You might ask, reader, how about Judas?)

Your thoughts cause you to lean back into the bush a bit too far, and you lose your balance. Stopping yourself from falling through creates quite a rustling commotion.

Regaining your balance, you can't resist peeking back through the bush one more time. The conversation appears to have quieted down a bit. Perhaps they're done? Pushing back the branches, you can make out the form of the bench the two men were seated on. The candle lanterns are still on the bench, but they are gone. Scanning to your left, then to your right, you see no trace of them.

The sound of gravel crackling under the weight of Judean sandals directly behind you releases an instant river of adrenaline coursing through your body, mainly because you know that the sound didn't come from beneath your own feet.

The firm grip of a hand grasping your shoulder confirms the release of a thousand butterflies in your now sickened stomach.

> THE FIRM GRIP OF A HAND GRASPING YOUR SHOULDER CONFIRMS THE RELEASE OF A THOUSAND BUTTERFLIES IN YOUR NOW SICKENED STOMACH. TURNING EVER SO SLOWLY ON THE HEELS OF YOUR SANDLES, YOU DISCOVER YESHUA AND NICODEMUS STANDING DIRECTLY BEHIND YOU.

Turning ever so slowly on the heels of your sandles, you discover Yeshua and Nicodemus standing directly behind you.

Yeshua asks, "Can we help you?"

Instantly you wish you could crawl under a leaf.

#

If you stopped reading the text of John 3 right at "For God so loved the world," without knowing anything more about Jesus's life and death, you would be as confused as you might be if you were eavesdropping from behind a bush that day, because Jesus was speaking of the task that was yet before Him.

Nicodemus was getting the idea.

Nicodemus came to Jesus at night, but he finally came into the light and identified with the Lord Jesus—who came as the Light to expose the darkness that men love so much.

If you, like our fictional bush-lurker, go home to do your own research and Torah study, you too will realize that Jesus was teaching about God's unconditional love for man, for you and for me! Then you realize that you have just been exposed to the greatest love story that has ever been written. Throw away those trashy romance novels, and grab hold of the greatest *unconditional* love story ever told! It's a love story based on God's goodness and grace, and God's grace is not all spent. The sun in our solar system will burn out long before the grace of God does … in fact, His grace will never burn out.

God is constantly trying to get through our resistance to prove His unconditional love for us. He dearly wants us to know that He hasn't placed any conditions on His love for us!

In fact, He loves even those who have rejected His Son as the Messiah. And it hurts Him that they have sentenced themselves, by their choice, to an eternity apart from God! He doesn't love them any less, nor does He love us any more just because we have chosen Jesus Christ, His Son, as appeasement for our sins!

> HE DOESN'T LOVE THEM ANY LESS, NOR DOES HE LOVE US ANY MORE JUST BECAUSE WE HAVE CHOSEN JESUS CHRIST, HIS SON, AS APPEASEMENT FOR OUR SINS!

This is the love of God:

No strings.

No attachments.

No conditions.

"Now there was a Pharisee, a man named Nicodemus who was a member of the Jewish ruling council. He came to Jesus at night and said, "Rabbi, we know that you are a teacher who has come from God. For no one could perform the signs you are doing if God were not with him." Jesus replied, "Very truly I tell you, no one can see the kingdom of God unless they are born again, from above."

John 3:1–3

"When Jesus spoke again to the people, he said, 'I am the light of the world. Whoever follows me will never walk in darkness, but will have the light of life.'"

John 8:12

Marinating Moments

1. Have you ever felt like murdering someone, like Moses did? Or perhaps, less violently, had resentment in yout heart toward someone? And then felt unworthy to speak to God because of your shame? If so, what does the record of the Torah and of Jesus's words say about your situation before God?

2. Has your faith ever waned after a great spiritual victory, and your self-defeated attitude wanted you to run, like Elijah? What was the end of that story for you? Did you encounter God in that wilderness? Have you ever asked God where He was in the midst of it?

3. Has our performance-based world caused you to believe that God only saves us or loves us based on performance for Him? What would Jesus say about that? Do you need to do an attitude check in your own heart and perhaps come to receive God's unconditional love for you?

Marinade 8:

The First Noel

"But you, Bethlehem, in the land of Judah, are by no means least among the rulers of Judah; for out of you will come a ruler who will shepherd my people Israel."

Matthew 2:6

To the shepherds standing guard in the grassy fields that form the outskirts of Bethlehem, there was no indication that anything other than the average cool evening was on tap. Another uneventful night was expected on the daily itinerary as the men watched over their slumbering flocks of sheep. Having assured themselves that the wolf, howling his contempt of the night, was at a safe distance from them, they hovered around the roaring campfire. The tips of the flames were rising high enough to lap at the bottom of the star-studded curtain of ebony blackness that hung over them like velveteen drapery. In their quiet discourse, they ignored the faint baby's cry that could be heard off in the distance.

Typically, as shepherds tended their flocks, small talk ruled the night. Although nothing unusual was scheduled or expected, this night was beginning to take on a shape that would forever change the course of history. In addition, its events would change these shepherds' lives forever. For this night, just outside of Bethlehem, the customary small talk had scaled up to swirling conversation,

FOR THE MOST PART, A SHEPHERD'S LIFE WAS QUITE BORING . . . NO BOOKS, NO TV, GAME BOY WAS A FEW YEARS AWAY. THERE WERE SIMPLY NO DISTRACTIONS BUT THE OCCASIONAL PREDATOR TO CHASE OFF.

all focused on the eerily brilliant celestial object that had mysteriously appeared overhead and had been shining day and night for some time now.

The object, which they determined was a star, was exceptionally brilliant and literally illuminated the night sky like a low-hanging moon. No one could recall when it showed up. Its brilliance served to chase the shadows, ordinarily relegated to lurking in darkness around the flock, to the uttermost edges of the horizon.

For the most part, a shepherd's life was quite boring … no books, no TV, Game Boy was a few years away. There were simply no distractions but the occasional predator to chase off. However, on this night there was this star, confidently hanging over the skies of Bethlehem, as if God Himself had willed it to be there. However, it didn't act like a normal star. There was no moving across the ecliptic plane, no rising, no setting. It was even visible during the day, resolutely hanging over Bethlehem with a purpose. What a conversation piece for lonely shepherds in a cool pasture on a not-so-common night!

Suddenly, with a swiftness that can only be likened to a cat's swat of her claws, their quiet night was shattered as an angel appeared on the scene. The best word to describe it was that the angel materialized in the air in front of them. As a result, the landscape glowed even more brightly than before. The glory of the Lord, as reflected by the angel's brilliance, was so intense that it caused the shepherds to shade their eyes as they cowered in fear. God had sent His calling card in the form of an angel to make a very special birth announcement.

As would be expected, common people didn't know how to act in the presence of an angel. Their ducking for cover alerted the angel to their fears. However, this radiant angel, sent from God, had comfort in his words for them; he had not come to frighten them or to harm them, but to make a birth announcement, and others would join him soon.

"Don't be afraid," his soothing, comforting voice assured them as they cowered, "because I have good news for you. It's the news that all Israel and mankind have been waiting for." He hesitated as the shepherds checked themselves and each other, looking for damage or wounds but noting that there hadn't been any harm done.

Now that he had their attention, he continued, "The long-awaited Messiah, yes, *the Messiah* has been born in Bethlehem."

What a marvelous scene this is! Through the words of an archangel, the Chief Shepherd has announced the birth of the Good Shepherd to the frightened shepherds. What an interesting development! Don't you find it fascinating how God unfolds His plans? The revealing of His Son drips with His logic!

WHAT A MARVELOUS SCENE THIS IS! THROUGH THE WORDS OF AN ARCHANGEL, THE CHIEF SHEPHERD HAS ANNOUNCED THE BIRTH OF THE GOOD SHEPHERD TO THE FRIGHTENED SHEPHERDS.

It is important to realize that these shepherds may have been frightened, but they were not dumb. As custom would have it, shepherds were not the most popular people in society. They were usually quiet and kept to themselves, pensive and meditating types; their job gave them plenty of time to think without distraction. Yet they knew the prophecies about the Messiah, and like mathematicians, they were adding two and two together.

Once assured that the shepherds were able to comprehend the scene, the angel continued his announcement: "For unto you is born this day in the City of David a Savior, which is Christ the Lord."

Note something interesting at this point: the angel says, "For unto *you,*" unto humanity, unto mankind, "a Savior is born." Angels don't need a savior, man does!

Man, adrift on a sea of sin, with no hope of seeing the promised land of eternal life with God in heaven, has just had his number called. Now, with the birth of the Savior (and the job yet to be done on the cross), man has his ticket to everlasting life with God. With the coming of the Messiah, man has been tossed the life preserver from the rails of the S.S. *Eternity*—with Jesus at the helm—and can be pulled to the promise of eternal safety. That is why Christ came: "For unto *us* a Savior is born."

Continuing on, the angel told the shepherds that they could go to the edge of town, behind the Bethlehem Inn, where the caretaker sheltered the animals of his guests, and they would locate the child. He would be identifiable by the fact that he would be lying in an animal's feeding trough.

In God's inimitable timing, the Messiah was finally unveiled— albeit rather humbly, in the extremely lowly surroundings of a barn. Couldn't God have cooked up something better than that?

One day, I was driving south along a major freeway in Southern California. The northbound lanes were eerily devoid of traffic. I thought that an accident must have shut down the northbound lanes further south of my position. Only a bad accident could have disrupted the northbound flow of traffic on this major artery through Los Angeles. Before long, though, I saw a couple of highway patrol motorcycle officers coming north, just two of them. Then, a mile or so behind them were about half-a-dozen highway patrol vehicles, two abreast, with lights and sirens blaring, filling all four lanes. Only yards behind their bumpers were three or four huge tourist-style sightseeing buses, followed by a few more police vehicles. Behind them was a huge wave of normal but congested traffic. I could only imagine the frustration in that group of cars. I later found out that I had observed the pomp and protection of a presidential candidate on his way to make a speech in the area. All this disruption for one man, and yet no fanfare or pomp for the King of Kings?

Just as suddenly as the first angel had materialized, a multitude of angels appeared in the same fashion and formed a heavenly choir, praising God as they sang, "Glory to God in the highest and on earth, peace, and goodwill toward men!"

> THE SAVIOR WAS FOR HUMANITY, NOT FOR THEM, YET THEY WERE REJOICING.

A heavenly choir rejoicing before men—on mankind's behalf! The Savior was for humanity, not for them, yet they were rejoicing. Oh, how that is such an example for us—to have joy and rejoicing when something good happens for others!

Remember Jonah? He was called, by God Himself, to minister God's message of love and salvation to the Ninevites, a people he considered the enemy. Reluctantly, and through a series of events that eventually convinced him to fulfill the mission, Jonah preached to the Ninevites. Within days, hundreds of thousands of Ninevites repented and turned to God. Nevertheless, that upset Jonah, because he would rather have seen them all perish. He didn't rejoice! The angels could be thinking the same way, but they aren't!

These angels were heralding the announcement of God's gift to humankind, who had entered the world to save sinners from themselves.

After the heavenly rejoicing ended and the angels dissolved back into their spiritual realm, the shepherds decided to follow instructions and check it out for themselves. So they raced into Bethlehem and went to the inn. Eventually they found Mary, Joseph, and the little baby Jesus, lying in a feeding trough as they had been told. An animal feeding trough, complete with grain remnants and bovine saliva.

> PERHAPS THE ANGELS ASSURED THEM THAT THEY WOULD WATCH THE FLOCKS FOR THEM SO THE SHEPHERDS COULD SEE FOR THEMSELVES, IN ESSENCE BECOMING ANGELIC "SHEEP-SITTERS."

These men, when heralded by the messengers

from God, dropped everything. Somehow, the flocks were disposed of, as the Bible says that "they came with haste." It is difficult to think they would abandon the flocks so readily. Perhaps the angels assured them that they would watch the flocks for them so the shepherds could see for themselves, in essence becoming angelic "sheep-sitters." It could also be that the angels appeared to these shepherds, and not to royalty like King Herod, because the animals they were watching were lambs that were ultimately going to be used as the sacrificial lambs in the temple ceremonies. Perhaps, just perhaps, the angels appeared to them because the ultimate "Lamb of God," who was going to eventually become the one sacrifice for all, had just arrived! The angels were announcing to these shepherds that their sheep were no longer going to be needed!

Meanwhile, back in Bethlehem, the shepherds ran into the stable, where they found Joseph, Mary, and baby Jesus, who was wrapped up in swaddling clothes just as the angels had announced, and when this all soaked into their minds, they hurried out and began shouting the news throughout the town. "The Messiah is born! Emmanuel, the Messiah, is here among us!"

That created a stir among the townsfolk. They wondered at the things these men were saying, and rightfully so, for they had been waiting for two thousand years for the Messiah to come.

Put yourself in the shoes of the townsfolk for a moment. They have waited all their lives, and for generations before them, for God to overthrow the effects of Satan and the bondage from sin that held them down. Was this it, finally? Was this really the long-awaited Messiah? So the townsfolk look out their windows, searching the street, looking for any sign of a police escort or a motorcade with Secret Service and marching bands and parades!

"But—wait!" you declare. "You mean to tell me He's lying in a feeding trough? In the musty old stable behind the inn? Where the common cow eats? It is at least a gold-lined manger, right? No? Bah, those kooky ol' shepherds; we never trusted them anyway. Let's go back to bed!"

While the shepherds were out stirring up the townsfolk, Mary remained with her son, pondering these events in her heart.

Every woman in Israel was hoping to be the one chosen by God to give birth to the Messiah, and here she was, reliving the time when the angel came to her and announced that she was the chosen one.

Just imagine the birth announcements:

IT'S A BOY!
Joseph and Mary, of Nazareth, are happy to announce the arrival of their
new baby boy in Bethlehem
Name: Immanuel
WT: 6 lbs. 5oz.
LGth: 21 inches
Penetrating brown eyes, wavy brown hair;
doesn't look much like Joseph;
but has a wonderful and charming smile.

However, it wasn't really new information. The angels only trumpeted what God, over the preceding centuries, had been revealing to man via preprinted birth announcements written by the prophets, including most of the specifics: the who, what, where, when, and how. (And yes, my friends, even the why.)

That night, in Bethlehem, God extended an eternal hand to mankind in the form of a free gift. He had said He would; years of prophetical writing, like an advance advertising campaign, spoke of this very night, proclaiming to humanity that the Messiah would arrive in this very way, in this very place, at this very time. Sadly, these were prophecies that humankind chose to ignore.

As the world around her buzzed with gossip, Mary was quietly seated, reflecting on all that she had been told and all that she had beheld.

The one thing that she was certain of, though, was that the Hebrew nation had been founded so that through them the whole

THAT NIGHT, IN BETHLE-
HEM, GOD EXTENDED AN
ETERNAL HAND TO MAN-
KIND IN THE FORM OF A
FREE GIFT. HE HAD SAID
HE WOULD; YEARS OF PRO-
PHETICAL WRITING, LIKE
AN ADVANCE ADVERTISING
CAMPAIGN, SPOKE OF THIS
VERY NIGHT, PROCLAIMING
TO HUMANITY THAT THE
MESSIAH WOULD ARRIVE
IN THIS VERY WAY, IN THIS
VERY PLACE, AT THIS VERY
TIME. SADLY, THESE WERE
PROPHECIES THAT HUMAN-
KIND CHOSE TO IGNORE.

world should be blessed. They were the Messianic nation to the world.

And there she was, in the City of David, the home of Ruth, Rachel's burying place. Just fifteen miles to the south was the home of Abraham, Isaac, and Jacob. Another six miles to the north was Jerusalem—the center of God's age-long effort to reveal His salvation message to humanity. And here she was with the hope of man and the promise of God cooing in her arms.

Her meditation was broken as the shepherds excitedly returned to the manger where Jesus lay.

That's where we'll leave the meditating Mary, the awestruck Joseph, the sleeping Jesus, and of course, the excited shepherds. We'll rejoin them in the next chapter.

#

THEY HAD JUST EXPERI-
ENCED A ONCE-IN-A-
LIFETIME—ONCE-IN-
AN-*ETERNITY*—
EXPERIENCE.

When the shepherds returned to their flocks in the field of Bethlehem, adrenaline continued to course through their bodies. Why not? They had just experienced a once-in-a-lifetime —once-in-an-*eternity*—experience.

"When the angels had left them and gone into heaven, the shepherds said to one another, 'Let's go to Bethlehem and see this thing that has happened, which the Lord has told us about.'"

Luke 2:15

"The shepherds returned, glorifying and praising God for all the things they had heard and seen, which were just as they had been told."

Luke 2:20

Marinating Moments

1. Imagine yourself seated in the manger alongside Mary, Joseph, and the animals. Knowing what Mary and Joseph knew about the newborn child, what do you think would be going on in your mind? Would you be in awe, or confusion?

2. All the words of the prophets have been fulfilled by this lone event in Bethlehem. Knowing that, how and what do you tell others about Jesus at Christmastime?

3. God gave us His gift, the gift of salvation through Jesus the Christ, from His heart to ours, because of His love for us. What comes to your mind when you think of the manger scene? Is there room for Jesus in the Inn of your heart? Or is he left out in the cold of your life?

Marinade 9:

The First Noel: Part 2

"But you, Bethlehem Ephrathah,
though you are small among the clans of Judah,
out of you will come for me
one who will be ruler over Israel,
whose origins are from of old,
from ancient times."

Micah 5:2

When we last left the stable, where Jesus was born, we saw Mary, Joseph, and their newly expanded family quietly resting after the excitement and activity of the birth. The quietness has now left them to their internal musings over the events.

Mary was pondering the things that had led up to this night, fondly and fearfully recalling the night the angel Gabriel came to her, informing her that she was to bear a child. Not just any child, but the Messiah of all mankind.

She remembered dreading how, and what, she was going to tell Joseph, to whom she was betrothed at the time.

Deep down she was still wondering what was going on. What did this all mean? How could she even really comprehend it?

Not far from Mary, we see Joseph staring at his little family, submerged in his own world of thought. He's deep in awestruck

NOT FAR FROM MARY, WE SEE JOSEPH STARING AT HIS LITTLE FAMILY, SUBMERGED IN HIS OWN WORLD OF THOUGHT. HE'S DEEP IN AWESTRUCK CONTEMPLATION.

contemplation. With emphasis on the word *awestruck*. How would you react, what would your thoughts be, if God placed the care of His only begotten Son into your hands? Imagine the questions, the fears, the uncertainties that were crossing through his mind! This man had been charged with raising the Son of God as his own. Were his thoughts different from Mary's? Were they of fear? Perhaps these were some of the things he was musing over:

Will I be teaching *Him* the Scriptures?

Will *He* be in the room when I pray?

Better yet, will *He* answer me?

When I teach *Him* the woodworking business, will *His* work have any flaws? Will *He* bend any nails?

Will *He* get blisters?

Will *He* have a scrap wood bin?

Will *He* ever hit His thumb with a hammer? If so, what words will fly out of *His* mouth?

There lies the Messiah (which means "anointed one"), the long-awaited King brought into the world that man might finally have that bridge that spans the chasm between Man and God—the chasm we call "sin." The one God had foreordained before the foundations of the world, given to this young couple to raise into manhood. Jesus is God, becoming man, to be raised by man, to be the savior of man—from man himself. Piece of cake, right?

And there He was, just lying there peacefully, looking up at Mom, cooing and making bubbles with his lips. Jesus, the Christ, the Anointed One, the Messiah, humbly lying in his mother's arms, wasn't just fussing for a meal. The baby, the one who represented the total focus of all the prophets through all the previous years, this baby, making little gurgling noises, was fulfilling hundreds of prophecies. All the hopes of mankind rested on the shoulders of this little fella. As Mary returned him to his makeshift bed, a stable's feeding trough, surrounded by a musty, damp, lousy old stable (remember there was no room for Him in the "Best Middle-Eastern Inn"), and covered by an atmospheric blanket of chilly air, He simply looked up at his parents in complete trust in their care for Him. Little did they comprehend that someday they would place their full trust in His eternal care for them!

He was born into a carpenter's family to become a craftsman, not only skilled at building things made of wood, but at the rebuilding of things made of the heart. In that particular trade, in fact, He was destined to be the Master Craftsman.

> LITTLE DID THEY COMPREHEND THAT SOMEDAY THEY WOULD PLACE THEIR FULL TRUST IN HIS ETERNAL CARE FOR THEM!

Yet, there He was, the King of Kings, the Lord of Lords, the mighty Counselor, the everlasting Father—suckling for milk.

God in diapers, cooing in a crèche!

Of course, in this same scene, there was an excited group of shepherds, who were running amok into the city and back to the stable again.

Michael Card catches the essence of this universal moment and helps us to understand the awe of Joseph in the words of his song "Joseph's Song":

> How could it be this baby in my arms
> Sleeping now, so peacefully
> The Son of God, the angel said
> How could it be
> Lord I know He's not my own
> Not of my flesh, not of my bone
> Still Father let this baby be
> The son of my love

Father show me where I fit into this plan of yours
How can a man be father to the Son of God
Lord for all my life I've been a simple carpenter
How can I raise a king, How can I raise a king
He looks so small, His face and hands so fair
And when He cries the sun just seems to disappear
But when He laughs it shines again
How could it be

THE TERM COMES FROM THE GREEK FORM OF A PERSIAN WORD *MAGOI*, WHICH IS USED TO IDENTIFY MEN WHO WERE EXPERTS IN STUDYING THE STARS OF THAT ERA.

Now, while all this was going on, the star, placed in the heavens by God, caught the attention of men in faraway lands, apparently including Babylon.

These men were intrigued and set out to follow the star. Because of tradition, and traditional Christmas songs, the men are known today as the "Wise Men," the "Three Kings," or the "Magi." The term comes from the Greek form of a Persian word *Magoi*, which is used to identify men who were experts in studying the stars of that era.

There are some interesting facts surrounding the Magoi:

1. There is no indication that they were three in number; it is most generally thought that there were actually quite a large entourage, because you wouldn't travel in those days, that distance, carrying gold and other costly items, through a gauntlet of marauding bandits in the desert, without a larger caravan of armed people.

2. There is no indication what country they were from; although it is usually thought to be Babylon. Much Hebrew literature and information about Messianic prophecies remained in the

land of Babylon after the Jewish captivity, and the Magoi do say that they were "in the East" when they saw the star and began to pursue the reason it hung where it hung—without movement—an astronomical anomaly for men who studied the mechanics of celestial movements.

3. There is no real indication that they were even kings. *Magoi* means "astrologer" more than it does "king." If "We Three Kings of Orient Are" is one of your favorite Christmas carols, this info may ruin it for you—sorry!

4. Whether they be kings or astrologers, you can take heart in this: they must have been high ranking enough in order to get access to King Herod!

5. They were expert in the study of the stars, so when they saw a new star, they coupled their astronomical knowledge with their apparent understanding of Numbers 24:17, where Balaam prophesies about a "Star out of Jacob," and they packed up their camels and headed out to worship the king.

Imagine the stir in Jerusalem as this huge entourage of visitors from a far-off land arrived with pomp and royal regalia. Couldn't you just see an actor, like a Peter Ustinov, playing the character of Herod? Herod, the paranoid king, who killed his own children so that they wouldn't plot to overthrow him (remember, it was said that it would be better to be one of Herod's pigs than one of his children).

Imagine the scene with me. This king, King Herod, is bounding back and forth, from one palatial window to the next, wondering who are these men, what do they want, are they here to overthrow him? *Maybe I should have them killed. No, looks like they have money with them. I'll see what they want,* then *I'll have them killed.*

The Magoi sent a message to Herod, inquiring as to where they could locate this newborn king of the Jews. An incendiary question indeed!

Before we look at this question's effect on Herod, however, here's an interesting thought to consider: the first question uttered in the Old

Testament is that of God inquiring of the first Adam, "Adam, where are you?" The first question in the New Testament is asked by the Magoi: "Where can we find the baby Jesus?", who is referred to by the apostle Paul in Romans as the "Second Adam." This time, man is asking of God, "Where are You?" And God will lead them straight to Himself.

Herod quickly gathers his Jewish religious leaders around him and demands of them whether the Scriptures say where the Messiah would be born, and they instruct him from Micah 5:2 that it was to be in Bethlehem.

These same religious leaders, who knew the birthplace of the Messiah and knew the prophecies concerning his arrival, later became Herod's worst enemies.

So Herod sends for the wise men to meet with him, the perfect gentleman (at least in front of them), and conforming to his new-found politeness, he proceeds to tell them that they will find the new-born king in Bethlehem. He even asks that they come back to him and "Ah, confirm that my religious leaders were right . . . yeah, that's it . . . come back to me simply to confirm our intelligence data. Perhaps I will go visit Him too!"

There was great anticipation surrounding the coming of the Messiah . . . there is even yet today.

Soon they were on their way toward Bethlehem, but not without subconsciously noting the tone of Herod's voice welcoming them back. The Scriptures tell us that they smelled a rat in Herod's attitude, and of course, that was aided by his reputation.

From the time they saw the star, made a pact to follow it, traveled to Jerusalem, inquired about Jesus, and caught up to His location, a year or so had elapsed, and the carpenter's family, including his stepchild, Jesus, were back in their home.

> THE SCRIPTURES TELL US THAT THEY SMELLED A RAT IN HEROD'S ATTITUDE, AND OF COURSE, THAT WAS AIDED BY HIS REPUTATION.

When the Magoi finally arrived, they worshiped Jesus as King of Kings … bowing to a one-year-old.

In addition, they offered Him precious commodities:

Gold—for His royalty.

Incense—for His deity.

Then they revealed the most interesting gift of all—myrrh. Why myrrh? After all, myrrh was an aromatic resin traditionally used as an embalming salve, set aside for a mortal man who has died. Yet, these men of science, from Babylon (Saddam Hussein territory), came all this way to worship this one-year-old as the King of Kings—using myrrh!

Just before they left Nazareth, God spoke to them in a dream and warned them not to go back to Herod, which confirmed their suspicions that Herod was up to no good.

After they left, an angel came to Joseph and instructed him to uproot his little family and flee to the safety of Egypt. On the heels of their departure, Herod put out the decree that all male children in Israel two years and younger were to be put to death … except that Jesus was already gone by then! Jesus was king by divine appointment: no mere mortal man was going to thwart God's plan!

This whole story surrounding the birth of Jesus, the Christ, is a grander picture of the world today.

We live with the expectation, the anticipation of someone who will come along and pull us out of this corrupt, sinful life in which we are trapped. Then Jesus comes along and asks us permission to take up residence in our hearts. That's amazing! More amazing is: some of us have a place for Him and some don't.

For those of us who don't, like Herod and the religious leaders, we spend the rest of our lives trying to destroy any evidence that He exists, so we won't have to be confronted by Him and the price He paid for our sins in the eyes of the Father and have to answer for it.

No matter how badly society wants to rid itself of Jesus the Christ, the data remains:

- Jesus was born of a virgin, as the Scripture foretold.
- Jesus led a sinless life so that we might have a role model and know that He understands and empathizes with our troubles.
- Without His birth, there would be no cross.
- Without the cross, there would be no atonement for our sins.
- Without His virgin birth, crucified death, and resurrection from the dead, there would be no salvation from the sins that beset us.

> WITHOUT HIS VIRGIN BIRTH, CRUCIFIED DEATH, AND RESURRECTION FROM THE DEAD, THERE WOULD BE NO SALVATION FROM THE SINS THAT BESET US.

> IF WE BELIEVE, WE WILL NOT PERISH.

If He had not come, we would have a right to feel depressed, or repressed, due to fears of the unknown.

However, the truth remains: because there was a virgin birth, there was a crucified death; because He is the only person to have ever been raised from the dead, we have God's promise from John 3:16. If we believe, we will not perish.

We do not await the arrival of the Anointed One's first visit to Planet Earth. Instead, we are awaiting His soon return, in which He is coming to claim us and take us to be with the Father in heaven. If you want to be on that flight, then take some time to commit your heart, your life, and your entire being to Him!

May we live for Christ boldly and, like the Magoi, seek Him and His grace.

"... Seek ye first the kingdom of God and His righteousness."

Matthew 6:33a (KJV)

Marinating Moments

1. How would you react, what would your thoughts be, if God placed the care of His only begotten Son into your hands to raise?

2. The Magoi brought costly gifts to worship a newborn king. What gave them confidence that their worship was not misplaced? What have you offered in worship to the Christ child? What gives you confidence that your worship is not misplaced?

3. Herod devoted his efforts to stamping out the work of God in his day, but his efforts were ultimately futile. In what ways do you see our society attempting to stamp out the work of God? To what end are their efforts destined?

Marinade 10:

The Gift of God

"In those days Caesar Augustus issued a decree that a census should be taken of the entire Roman world."

Luke 2:1

At the mall, the week before Chrsitmas . . . what was I thinking!

All the hustling and bustling about ... the time of year where it seems that someone has been handing out licenses legalizing pure shopping insanity!

Walking through the mall, I felt as if I had entered a fishbowl, as I was immediately caught up in a teeming school of people flowing mindlessly from storefront to storefront. I felt that I had gotten there at feeding time; it was like someone had tossed in some raw meat and I had entered into the middle of a feeding frenzy. People were running around with large lists of names, checking them off as they tossed new packages of matchbox toys and underwear in their carts.

I saw mothers asking their children, "Won't Daddy like this?"

The shrill answers came: "No, Mommy! I wanna give 'im this!" However, Mom responded, with a bit of firmness and an "I know better" tone of voice, "Yes, he would . . ." and tossed her choice in the cart anyway, concluding, "It'll be from you, sweetheart," flashing a halfhearted smirk of victory over the child.

> AND ON AND ON AS THE SHOCK WAVE SETS IN! THE SHOPPERS' FEAR IS WRITTEN ALL OVER THEIR FACES AND CAN BE SEEN THROUGH THEIR EYES AS THEY MARCH IN RYTHYM, AS IF SOMEONE IS GOING TO TAKE THEIR LIVES IF THEY'RE FORGOTTEN AT CHRISTMAS.

Then there were the daddies. It's fun to watch the guys who are never in the mall during the year, especially when they get to that one certain part—you know the place; the place where they run past the door of Victoria's Secret so they won't be seen near it! "I wasn't in that store . . . I-I-I wasn't even looking!"

Ah, but then there are the panic-stricken ones. It's written all over their faces: "What do I get for her? What do I get Aunt Sue and Uncle George … and there's Sally at the office … and there's … and there's …" And on and on as the shock wave sets in! The shoppers' fear is written all over their faces and can be seen through their eyes as they march in rythym, as if someone is going to take their lives if they've forgotten at Christmas.

So many bitten by the same shopping virus. It honestly makes you wonder: what was the scene like in heaven, so many years ago? (Please don't think I am being irreverent here.)

Think about it for a moment. Allow yourself the opportunity to eavesdrop into heaven some two thousand years ago. There's God, muttering to Himself over in the corner of the room; rustling about in the closest; mumbling. Your hearing sharpens as you get closer, and you actually hear God reviewing His Christmas gift list. "Um, let's see, what am I going to get my little angels? Michael's first on the list; I'll get him a new set of glorious wings. He'll be trying them out soon."

He continues, "Now there's, oh yeah, Gabriel. Ha! Great idea, I'll get him a shiny new trumpet. He'll be needing it to announce the coming king. Now, who am I forgetting? Yes, I thought so, Lucifer. Oh my, there's this naughty-or-nice thing to deal with. Well, that settles it, a box of ashes for that rebellious young fellow."

Thinking He's done, you begin to back away when you hear Him exclaim, "Oh, wait, there's one more on the list; there's Mankind! What could I possibly get Mankind? Well, let's see, how about my creation, Earth, adorned with colorful trees and flowers and animals. Hmmm, no, they'll worship that. Maybe I could get them an automobile ... no, they'll worship that ... maybe I could get them a TV ... no, they'll worship that too. Let's see; I could get them a fine leader ... no, they'll worship him and set him up as a king. *I'm King!*"

The thoughts are whizzing through God's head and He's speaking them aloud. "What do I get for people who are going to an eternal torment in hell? What are their basic needs? What can I possibly do that won't be forcing Myself on them? I want to give them a gift that will give them the opportunity of choice they so adamantly clamor for. I want to get them a gift that shows that I really care, a gift that demonstrates that I genuinely love them. One that I have thoroughly thought out. Hummmmm, let's see, I've got it . . . Jesus, can You step over here for a moment? I need to speak to You, please."

#

Now, we well know that particular scene didn't really play out in heaven, because the Bible tells us that God knew before He even made the world that He was going to provide *Himself* a sacrifice! (Genesis 22:14.)

Let's take a look at how God gives gifts.

We cover familiar terrain as we read the nativity account of Dr. Luke, chapter 2, a very well-read and well-known portion of Scripture, especially at Christmastime. However, so often something gets missed as we read the account of Christ's birth. There are some obvious and not so obvious points that we should review.

> THE BIBLE TELLS US THAT GOD KNEW BEFORE HE EVEN MADE THE WORLD THAT HE WAS GOING TO PROVIDE *HIMSELF* A SACRIFICE!

Looking back at Luke 2:1, we see a small hint of the details God took into account as He thought this gift out. We can stop off at all sorts of waypoints to uncover God's thought-out gift to us. For instance, what's so special about verse 2:2—"And this taxing was first made when Cyrenius was governor of Syria?" For many, many years this particular text was a troublesome one becasue it didn't add up date wise with history as we knew it. It wasn't well-known that there was a second tax decree when Cyrenius was governor of Syria. As it turns out, the shovel of the archeologist saves the day. Recently discovered papyri noted that Cyrenius was govenor: twice! Dr. Luke notes that this was his first tax decree. That little detail in the account gives us the ability, thousands of years later, to accurately locate Jesus's birth in history, warding off those who believe there are inaccuracies in the biblical account and offering us one more reason for our solid faith!

> THE FIRST CHRISTMAS GIFT OF GOD TO MAN WAS SENT SPECIAL DELIVERY TO BETHLEHEM.

The predicted and prophesied Messiah was delivered to mankind all wrapped up as the first Christmas present ever presented (albeit in swaddling clothes). The first Christmas gift of God to man was sent special delivery to Bethlehem.

Another thoughtful detail: the royal Jesus in His not-so-royal surroundings, the King of Kings, the Lord of Lords, responding to the mooing of the cows and the bleating of the sheep … why wasn't He born in a palace like all the other kings? Why a stable? Why is his first crib a trough animals eat from and slobber on?

> WHY A STABLE? WHY IS HIS FIRST CRIB A TROUGH ANIMALS EAT FROM AND SLOBBER ON?

Here's a possible answer: who can relate to royalty? Only those of royal bloodlines. More of us—nearly all of us!—can relate to a king who was born in rough circumstances, one who has "been there, done that." Whatever it is that you are going through, how can an earthly king relate to that unless he has had those humble beginnings? You see, God has even thought that part out!

The sleepy-eyed shepherds get to play a role here also. There they were, minding their own sheep-tending business, probably watching over the sheep that were going to be used in the temple sacrifices, when all of a sudden, in what was the first Christmas choir program in history, the angels were telling them in their own way that they could let the sheep go—temple sacrifices wouldn't be required any longer, as the Lamb of God had been born in Bethlehem. In fact, the angels urge them, go in and see Him!

In the meantime, God manuevered the heavens to allow the appearance of a brilliant celestial object (a star?) so dazzling that it would draw men from the East to come visit. It's interesting to note that as they arrived, they too had gifts … they brought gifts to the Gift!

> IT'S INTERESTING TO NOTE THAT AS THEY ARRIVED, THEY TOO HAD GIFTS … THEY BROUGHT GIFTS TO THE GIFT!

Something stirs inside us as we see their gifts for Jesus. What did they know that the others didn't? Did they know the prophetic Scriptures so well that their gifts reflected their knowledge and understanding of them?

They brought Him gold. Fine, gold was a symbol of His kingly role.

They brought frankincense. Okay, it's a very expensive incense that symbolized His priestly role and even his divinity.

But interestingly enough, they also brought myrrh. Why myrrh? After all, as we've already noted, myrrh was used for embalming the dead. What did they know about this Gift to mankind?

In the movie *The Christmas Box,* the plot centers around mankind getting the purpose of God's gift to man. A recurring question brought up in the movie is, "What was the first gift given at Christmas?" And while the young man in the movie flippantly says "Love," he is only partially right.

But then he discovers that the first gift given at Christmas was Jesus: because of love! Then he reads John 3:16, and it all comes together for him:

> For God so loved the world, that He gave His only begotten Son, that whosoever believes in Him should not perish but have everlasting life.

The famous John 3:16! (KJV)

GOD LOWERED HIMSELF SO THAT MAN MIGHT BE LIFTED UP.

God gave the first Christmas present ever, and it wasn't wrapped in shiny paper nor tied up with a bow, but wrapped in swaddling strips of cloth, in a barn, in an animal's feeding trough. God lowered Himself so that man might be lifted up.

And man! Did God think this one out! His is a gift that is really many gifts wrapped in one. With one gift, we receive so many gifts. Here are a few:

First—We receive the gift *of* God. In John 4:10, Jesus was speaking to the lady at the well, and He asked her for water. When she hesitated and began to argue with Him, He said, "If thou knewest the gift of God, and who it is that saith to thee, give me to drink; thou wouldest have asked of him, and he would have given thee living water."

Second—We receive the gift of salvation. As we mentioned before regarding John 3:16, God's gift of His Son allows us to receive the gift of salvation.

Third—We receive the gift of faith. Ephesians 2:8 says, "For it is by grace you have been saved, through faith—and this is not from yourselves, it is the gift of God." Paul tells us that by grace we are saved through *faith* . . . which is a gift from the Gift!

Fourth—We receive the gift of the Holy Spirit. In Acts 2:38 we read, "Peter replied, 'Repent and be baptized, every one of you, in the name of Jesus Christ for the forgiveness of your sins. And you will receive the gift of the Holy Spirit.'"

Fifth—We receive various gifts from the Holy Spirit. "God also testified to it by signs, wonders and various miracles, and by gifts of the Holy Spirit distributed according to his will" (Hebrews 2:4).

Do your own word study on the "gift of God," and you will see the many, many gifts from the one Gift swaddled in a manger—the gift of Jesus the Christ!

There's something very significant about gifts. When you offer one, you usually don't expect to reveal the cost. This past Christmas, I found myself concentrating on removing the price tags off the packages as I was wrapping them . . . sometimes because I didn't want people to know how *little* I had paid! It made me think that God was not ashamed to tell us that His gift to us cost Him dearly. His Son, hanging on a cross, dying in our place, for us to refuse or accept—this was a very costly gift!

Romans 6:23 says, "For the wages of sin is death; but the gift of God is eternal life through Jesus Christ our Lord!" (KJV)

On Christmas Eve or Christmas morning, we'll be spending time shredding wrapping paper to bits, tearing into boxes that have been so carefully wrapped ... and we will be so absorbed into ourselves. "What am *I* getting?" "Oh *I* can't wait . . . O-O-O." Sadly, very few of us will even think about the gift that was placed in a manger, wrapped in dull, unadorning covers.

Even sadder though is that the gift of God will be left unopened by many! In so many people's lives, it is usually the last one remaining under the tree. The thought is that maybe someday, I'll reach for it and open it up. For some people, "someday" never comes.

> BUT THE GIFT OF GOD IS ETERNAL LIFE THROUGH JESUS CHRIST OUR LORD!

Have you ever had a gift given to you that left you speechless? One that was indescribable? One that clamped your jaw tight and you just couldn't say anything? If you did not react the same way to the gift of Jesus, perhaps it's because you haven't recognized the value of this gift of God.

What value is there in this gift of eternal life? Well, let's say you received a tie for Christmas, valued at about twenty dollars. Or you received a diamond bracelet, valued at three hundred dollars. However, some of you received a Boeing 787 Dreamliner, valued at two hundred million dollars. Each of these items has a price relative to its market value. But what about Jesus? What would His relative market value be? What price or relative market value does eternal life in heaven have? One thing is for sure—everybody will receive "eternal life," but not everybody will spend it in the same place!

> ONE THING IS FOR SURE—EVERYBODY WILL RECEIVE "ETERNAL LIFE," BUT NOT EVERYBODY WILL SPEND IT IN THE SAME PLACE!

The apostle Paul describes this as an "unspeakable, jaw-dropping, off the charts" kind of gift (2 Corinthians 9:15). Remember, this is the same Paul/Saul of Tarsus, who was killing people who had accepted that same gift in their lives. Now, the penitent Paul is praising the gift as the gift to beat all gifts!

In that humble beginning, in a stable sprinkled with straw and crowded with curious onlookers, glowing candles over in the corner cast a foreboding shadow. Along with the shadows of cows and sheep and people, stood the ominous shadow of the cross. A shadow that the young Christ would always see as He looked over His shoulder. From the crèche to the cross, He is the gift of God to mankind.

\#

The tree is taken down; the last pieces of pine needles and tinsel have been vacumed up; this year's Christmas melee is over

... but in some people's lives, there remains one solitary Gift left unopened.

The gift of life . . . eternal life.

A costly, precious gift . . . expensive because it was paid for not with money, but with a life!

The tree is gone, all remnants of Christmas have been stored away until next year, the season is all wrapped up, except for the one gift that remains. And God wonders, what will it take?

If you and I were to see a gift left under the tree for someone we loved, a gift that we had thought out, paid a dear price for, lovingly wrapped up and offered unconditionally, and the recipient refused it because they simply didn't want to surrender all the fun of their lifestyle ("You mean give up the fun of my measly seventy years on earth for eternity in heaven? Sounds like religion. No way!"), you and I would walk away dejected. Perhaps even feeling rejected. Shucks, maybe we'd even reach out and take the gift back and say, "I'll just give it to someone who really deserves it, or someone who will appreciate it better. I'll show you!"

But not God!

He continues to patiently hold out the gift to all who will receive it. Now is best! Later is okay. But to refuse is disaster.

During the Christmas season, don't be fooled by jolly old men in red pajamas. Instead, remember the gift of God, a gift that has many gifts that come with it. Truly a gift that keeps giving!

And give God a gift in return ... *your* heart and your life! Why not? He's already paid for it. That's tanatamount to me handing my son some cash and asking him to buy me a gift with it, then saying it's from him!

> MAN CANNOT FULLY FATHOM THE VALUE OF WHAT GOD GIVES. THE GOSPEL IS A GOSPEL OF GIVING AND FORGIVING. YOU CAN SUM IT ALL UP IN THESE FEW WORDS: "TO WHOM GOD GIVES FREELY, HE ALSO FORGIVES."

Man cannot fully fathom the value of what God gives. The gospel is a gospel of giving and forgiving. You can sum it all up in theses few words: "To whom God gives freely, He also forgives."

This wasn't a one-time, soon-to-be tossed gift, but one that had a destiny. Can there be any more perfect a gift than the one God has given us? He was born to die. The amazing purpose of His birth was that He was born solely to become a sacrifice.

Jesus represents to us a gift from God that hasn't worn out, will never wear out, won't rust, won't break, won't need replacement parts or spark plugs. It is a gift that continues to give life and hope to the downcast, the downtrodden, and the joyous alike.

Amazingly, for all its joy and glory and angels singing, this story had a sad beginning that leads to an equally sad ending as far as stories of human adventures go. Inasmuch as there was no room for Joseph and the soon-to-deliver Mary in the Bethlehem Inn, in essence no room for the Messiah, in the same way the world treats Jesus today. No room for the Messiah. The world has crowded Him out. There is time for business. There is time for pleasure. But there is no time for Jesus.

It would behoove us to ask ourselves today: have we left room in our hearts and in our holiday celebrations for Jesus? So often, I fear that if we were to search through the morning-after-Christmas wrapping paper, there, shoved in the trash can along with the crumpled paper and the torn bows would be Jesus, because He wasn't the center of the celebration.

What can you say about such a gift: it's unspeakable, it's indescribable! The gift of God becomes the hope of humanity! Doesn't that make you stop and think about the magnitude of such a gift, and wonder about the God who provided it? *The gift of life, in exchange for the life of the gift!*

"Thanks be to God for his indescribable gift!"

2 Corinthians 9:15

Marinating Moments

1. In your own study time, grab a concordance and go through the Bible to see if you can find all the mentions of "gift" or "gifts." How many of them tie to God as the gift-giver? Have you received these gifts from Him?

2. What is it that is crowding Christ from your life? During the holidays in particular, what pushes Him out? Do these things hold true throughout the year? What can you do to change that?

3. Search through the Scriptures and discover five verses that speak of God's love for us. Write them down. Be prepared to meditate on them or share them with the group.

Marinade 11:

Resurrection Sunday

"After the Sabbath, at dawn on the first day of the week,
Mary Magdalene and the other Mary went to look at
the tomb."

Matthew 28:1

It was a crisp and chilly morning that seventeenth day of Nisan, the first day of the week. The roosters were crowing in the distance as they heralded the approach of a new day just as the sun crested the eastern horizon.

In two different homes, two separate glowing candlewicks were chasing the predawn darkness back into the dim corners of the room. In two separate houses, two separate women were preparing for the same daunting task, both sharing the same mourning sentiments, triggered by the same tragic events that had transpired just three days prior, as they mutually awaited the rising of the sun.

For them, and many of their friends, life as they had known it for the past three and a half years had come to a dead stop. They were moping around in a completely meaningless existence. For them life was not worth living any longer. Their hopes had been smashed like a ripe watermelon crashing on a rock.

Two women, two Marys—Mary Magdalene and Mary, the mother of James, Joses and Jesus—both paced anxiously with their spikenard,

> **THEY WERE MOPING AROUND IN A COMPLETELY MEANINGLESS EXISTENCE.**

aloe, myrrh, and other traditional embalming spices in hand. Their intent was to meet up and complete the painful and unrewarding process of embalming Jesus's lifeless body. They would have done it yesterday, but the law of the Sabbath prevented them.

Patiently they waited, yet they were both determined, and inspired, to beat the early shards of the sun's rays to the most famous sepulcher in human history—the tomb where Jesus's body lay. All the while attempting to chase the thoughts of that frightful Friday out of their memories. That, however, was proving to be an insurmountable task. Both women were replaying the imagery of the scenes they had endured on Friday, scenes which served only to haunt them.

Swirling in their mind's eye were images of the limp body of Jesus hanging on the cross in the heat of the midday sun and the Roman soldiers mocking Him. Moreover, the recurring sounds of the taunts of the angry crowd still echoed in their ears. All were mercilessly repeating over and over again. Meanwhile, the authorities were trying to figure out what to do amidst the chaos of that unforgettable Friday afternoon.

> **RIGHT AROUND NOON THAT DAY, ALL HELL SEEMED TO BREAK LOOSE AS GOD'S FURY WAS UNLEASHED AT A MOMENT'S NOTICE.**

Right around noon that day, all hell seemed to break loose as God's fury was unleashed at a moment's notice. What an ironic scene was playing out on the universal stage!

Jesus was God manifest in the flesh.

God become a man to save man from himself.

God, being crucified by the men He was coming to rescue.

Grace, being demonstrated in such a horrible symbol of death.

Meanwhile, apparently unnoticed by the people determined to rid the world of Jesus, an amazing astronomical event brought unexplainable darkness all over the land. Some have claimed that it was a total solar eclipse. However, scientifically, it is known that the longest any one area of earth could be subject to the darkness of a solar eclipse would only be six to seven minutes. On this one dreadful Friday, it remained dark for three hours.

As the sky inexplicably darkened, another event was taking place. An earthquake trembled beneath their feet—yet another phenomenal aspect of the day that they had to deal with mentally.

As if that wasn't enough to grasp intellectually or try to explain, when Jesus gave up His Spirit and was immediately in the presence of the Father, there were others walking the streets … others, that is, who had emerged from their graves. Formerly dead people, now walking the streets of Jerusalem once again! Imagine that sight! People whom you buried are now walking around the highways and byways of Israel again.

Additionally, there was an immediate investigative team sent to the temple mount to find, capture, and prosecute the vandals who tore the veil in the temple. How were they able to gain access to the top of the veil—the one that separated the rest of the temple from the Holy of Holies, where the ark of the covenant, the mercy seat, and other holy objects lay in state? How could anyone possibly tear it from the top of the veil to the bottom? As a result of this heinous act of vandalism, the Holy of Holies, a place that only the high priest was allowed to enter (and that only once a year) had been violated and laid bare, exposed for all common men to see. This was not just some cheap peek, as if someone had just pulled the curtain back and dared others to see. No, it was literally ripped in half! Who would do this dastardly deed?

How would God tolerate this? What horrible wrath would descend upon mankind from heaven?

The mysteries of the day were piling up. But for those with eyes to see— today as on that fateful

THE MYSTERIES OF THE DAY WERE PILING UP.

day itself—the tearing of the temple veil wasn't meant as a display of power, but to send a message to all people for the many lessons that are to be learned from this incident.

Like what, you ask? What lessons need to be learned?

First, in God's eyes, the old law of ordinances has now been put away. As Jesus surrendered His Spirit, the official transfer of Jesus's Spirit from the cross to the throne completed the temple sacrifices forever in God's sight. God considered them as finished, because no future sacrifices were going to be needed. They were now all fulfilled through Christ's determination on the cross. God sees this once and final sacrifice as atoning for all, forever. The atoning blood which was once annually sprinkled within the veil has been offered once for all by the sacrificial Lamb provided by God Himself, whose blood was splashed all over the cross. No blood of bulls or lambs is needed anymore, because Jesus has entered within the veil, within the Holy of Holies, and has covered it with His sanctified blood.

Second, the torn veil revealed all the hidden things about the Holy of Holies. The mercy seat could now be seen by everybody, and the glory of God brilliantly shone forth, flooding the temple mount with God's shekinah glory. Because of Christ, things that have been hidden since the foundations of the world are revealed for all of mankind to see and to experience.

A very striking verse emerges from Romans 10:4: "For Christ is the end of the law for righteousness to everyone that believes." Christ has freed us from the law of Moses, because in Him the law has been made complete. The logic would be that since we are in Him, and He is in us, we have therefore fulfilled the law also, by the very virtue of our spiritual connection with Jesus.

As we've already seen, the torn veil wasn't a tiny slit in a curtain for some cheap peek at the mercy seat nestled atop the ark of the covenant. It was a gaping separation, a totally ripped curtain which allows us the opportunity to come boldly before the throne of God Himself! In effect, the torn veil has become a door that Jesus has opened and no man can sew shut. No matter how much people want to disbelieve in the existence of God, no matter how much thread they use to try to sew the veil shut, they cannot undo the work Jesus has done on our behalf.

Darkness, earthquakes, the walking dead, and the apparent "desecration" of the temple—those were just a few of the things to deal with on the day Jesus died. Surely, God was expressing His opinion over the rejection of His Son by mankind!

> AS WE'VE ALREADY SEEN, THE TORN VEIL WASN'T A TINY SLIT IN A CURTAIN FOR SOME CHEAP PEEK AT THE MERCY SEAT NESTLED ATOP THE ARK OF THE COVENANT. IT WAS A GAPING SEPARATION, A TOTALLY RIPPED CURTAIN WHICH ALLOWS US THE OPPORTUNITY TO COME BOLDLY BEFORE THE THRONE OF GOD HIMSELF!

Over the years, people have asked: why? Why would Jesus do such a thing? Why would God pay such a price? The answer is found in His love for us. As your circumstances want to overwhelm you, as your life seems to be tossed upside down, as people treat you badly and use and abuse you, Jesus can pull you close to Himself and say, "I know, I know … those creeps … I know what you're going through, because I've been there!" He's acquainted with our griefs, He knows our sorrows. He's been there, done that!

People ask, and rightfully so: "Why didn't He come down from the cross?" The answer is as simple as it is complex: had He come down from the cross, several things would have happened, and several others wouldn't have happened:

1. Had He come down, the people still would not have believed that He was the Son of God. He would have vindicated Himself as a prophet, but unbelievers would not have been won over.

2. If He had saved Himself, He could not have saved others, and our faith would be in vain.

> BUT THE TORN VEIL, THE EARTHQUAKES, THE DARKENED SKIES WOULD MEAN NOTHING IF, ON SUNDAY MORNING, THE TWO MARYS HAD ARRIVED AT A TOMB FULL OF JESUS'S REMAINS.

But the torn veil, the earthquakes, the darkened skies would mean nothing if, on Sunday morning, the two Marys had arrived at a tomb full of Jesus's remains.

Today, if I visit my mother's grave in Southern California, I am assured that her remains are still there. Hers is an occupied grave. That's why they call them "remains." However, there were no remains in Jesus's tomb.

The empty tomb is our sign of hope. The cross reminds us of the completion of the law and of God's merciful grace to convicted sinners. While the cross speaks of the end of our slavery to sin and the grip of death, the empty tomb speaks to us of the hope that we have in an eternity with Christ in heaven.

Billy Graham has written: "There is more evidence that Jesus rose from the dead than there is that Julius Caesar ever lived or that Alexander the Great died at the age of thirty-three."

Resurrection Sunday is more important than the events of Good Friday afternoon. Here are four things to keep in mind on the next Resurrection Sunday:

First, Resurrection Sunday assures us of our own future resurrection. Because Jesus died and rose again, we too shall one day be raised like Him (1 Thessalonians 4:13–18). In fact, the entire structure of the Christian faith rests upon the foundation of the resurrection. If we do away with His resurrection, we do away with our hope.

Second, Christ's resurrection is the basis for His heavenly priesthood. Because He lives by the power of an endless life, He is able to save us "to the uttermost" (Hebrews 7:23–28).

Third, the resurrection gives us power for Christian living. We cannot live for God by our own strength. It is only as His resurrection power works in and through us that we can do His will and glorify His name. This is what Romans chapter 8 is all about!

Fourth, Resurrection Sunday assures us of our future inheritance. Because we have a living Savior, we hope! Because He lives, we experience hopeful living. A fading hope grows weaker and weaker before it eventually dies—but Jesus Christ is alive! Therefore, we have a glorious future!

Mankind—wise, yet foolish mankind— thought they had defeated this Jesus character by nailing Him to a cross. They envisioned that their grand schemes and shrewd planning to kill Him and

> MANKIND—WISE, YET FOOLISH MANKIND—THOUGHT THEY HAD DEFEATED THIS JESUS CHARACTER BY NAILING HIM TO A CROSS.

bury Him would take care of Him, His band of believers, and the revolutionary movement He had started forever!

However, death could not hold Him. No tomb on earth could seal Him in.

Even as the earthquake rattled the hill at Calvary, even as nighttime's darkness filled the sky, even as the veil in the temple was being torn by God's majestic hand, the victory crown was being handed to the victor. Jesus, the Christ, was opening the door for mankind to His Father in heaven. That lone act of selfless love stands forever: "Greater love has no one than this: to lay down one's life for one's friends" (John 15:13).

For God so loved the world that He gave His only begotten Son, that whosoever should believe in Him should not die a spiritual death, but have everlasting spiritual life! And Jesus, the Christ, accomplished that task on the old rugged cross back on that terrible day in April, AD 33.

One question remains:

What have you done about Jesus?

John Wesley wrote: "Jesus is risen! He shall the world restore! Awake, ye dead! Dull sinners, sleep no more!"

As a young man, D.L. Moody was called upon suddenly to preach a funeral sermon. He hunted all throughout the four Gospels trying to find one of Christ's funeral sermons, but He searched in vain. He found that Christ broke up every funeral He ever attended. Death could not exist where He was. When the dead heard His voice, they sprang to life. Jesus said, "I am the resurrection and the life" (John 11:25a).

> THE BIBLE IS CLEAR: *EVERY-BODY GETS ETERNITY!* HOWEVER, NOT EVERYBODY GETS TO SPEND ETERNITY IN THE SAME PLACE.

Today is *your day* of resurrection: even today, you can change the path that your eternity is headed down. The Bible is clear: *everybody gets eternity!* However, not everybody gets to spend eternity in the same place. Despite what the world and the movies teach us, we are not all destined for heaven. Those who are Christless, by their own choice, will receive the inheritance of pain and wailing and gnashing of teeth, always regretting their choice.

How many times do we hear ignorant people say, "Aunt Martha is looking down on us from heaven"? How come we never hear, "Aunt Martha is looking up …"? That would infer that Aunt Martha, God bless her soul, is in hell looking up at us. Nobody wants to think that there is a hell, or that sweet Aunt Martha could possibly be there! Much of our culture is engaged in wishful thinking about the afterlife. But for those who choose the reality of the empty tomb, they will know the joy and the peace and the hope that the Good News of Resurrection Sunday brings.

\#

Perhaps as you read this, you have sensed the Holy Spirit tugging on your heart, even now. So far, as you have read through this book, you have been feeling a strange disconnect from your life. It's one of those times when you say "I don't want to know any more," yet you're having trouble putting the book down because something is compelling you to read on!

That, my friend, is the work of the Holy Spirit drawing you to the Lord. He is calling you to be at home with Christ. All it takes is your surrendered spirit. Place it trustingly into the hands of Christ, and then relax. You are now a citizen of heaven!

#

The two Marys, both pacing the floor of their homes, both awaiting the sunrise, did not realize that the Son *had* risen, just as He said He would. Funny thing was, He was awaiting *their* arrival: to greet them, to hug them, to love them, to assure them. They waited, and He waited. It's the story of man: Jesus is waiting to receive man, but man is pacing, hesitating. All the while, He waits for us.

Jesus awaits our arrival with tender hugs and unbounding love. He is ready with His arms wide open to wrap around us and say, "Well done, my good and faithful servant."

> JESUS AWAITS OUR ARRIVAL WITH TENDER HUGS AND UNBOUNDING LOVE.

I want Him to say that to me. "My good"— and I trust that He will add to my account— "and faithful servant"

How about you?

*"For as in Adam all die, even so in Christ shall
all be made alive."*

1 Corinthians 15:22 (KJV)

Marinating Moments

1. What have you done about Jesus the Christ in your life? Have you made your confession of faith and trust in Him? If not, what's stopping you from doing it today?

2. What evidence do you have of your eternal address? When you die, will your forwarding address be heavenly or hellish?

3. "Good and faithful servant": are those words going to welcome you to your in eternity? How do you know?

Marinade 12:

Four Reasons He Didn't Come Down

"For the joy set before him he endured the cross, scorning its shame, and sat down at the right hand of the throne of God."

Hebrews 12:2b

The hill is called Golgotha, and it's located just northwest of the temple mount in Jerusalem. You find yourself mingling around with the spectators because this Jesus character has held a particular interest to you. In the past couple of years, you've seen His many wonderful works and heard of miracles that were purportedly produced by Him. Those incidents helped convince you of His sincerity, His genuineness, His humanity, but not necessarily His deity. After all, you've seen magicians perform sleight of hand and all, so you remain skeptical.

After shaking a few pieces of gravel out of your sandals, you walk around to the other side of the crowd that is blocking your view to get a better look. There is a lot of activity on the ground in front of the two other crosses. The horde of onlookers, including the ones who are partially blocking your view, are ranting and jeering and hurling insulting remarks at the activity in front of them.

THEN, WITH A UNIVERSAL GASP OF THE CROWD, IT EMERGES RIGHT IN FRONT OF YOU. THE GIANT PILLORY BEING LIFTED UP BY THE ROMAN SOLDIERS BECOMES THE THIRD CROSS—THE CENTER ONE—AS IT TAKES ITS PLACE BETWEEN THE OTHER TWO.

Then, with a universal gasp of the crowd, it emerges right in front of you. The giant pillory being lifted up by the Roman soldiers becomes the third cross—the center one—as it takes its place between the other two. As the soldiers tip it up above the crowd, you see clearly what all the jeers and hostility were about. Being raised high up into the air is Him … the man from Galilee. The same man who only days ago walked the highways and byways of Judea and Samaria, healing the sick and counseling the hurting, is now being constrained by manmade manacles.

A cacophony of sounds and jeering noises fill the air all around you. The mockers are there to taunt and wave accusing fingers, as people have been prone to do throughout the centuries. The soldiers themselves are just fulfilling their orders. Mixed into all the confusion are tears and jeers. However, because of your interest in this man, there is one jeer that you keep hearing in the background that is affecting you the most. It is stirring, haunting, and perhaps the most profound and logical jeer of them all. Your own built-in filter isn't allowing you to equalize this one jeer with the others.

But don't worry, you're in good company, because Matthew heard it too. Mark was there; he couldn't escape it. In addition, John didn't miss it either. From whatever their vantage points, these three men heard the same taunt, and all of them wrote about it.

They weren't exactly surrounded by friends at the time. Most of His disciples suddenly called in sick once they learned that the government had apprehended their Galilean trailblazer. But the three remaining disciples heard it and thought it important to write it down.

Today, I still hear it—all too often. Sometimes it comes from relatives, or friends, or coworkers … and it is indeed a nagging question, bouncing around in the mind like a ricocheting bullet.

Why doesn't he come down from there?

You can hear one of the other malefactors on a cross to your right, through clenched teeth, demand it: "Come down from your cross; come down from that shame. Save yourself! If you are who you say you are, the so-called Son of God, then do yourself a favor to prove your case—come down off of there!" Others on the ground are praying, "Oh Jesus, please, prove Yourself; prove that You are who You say You are; You are what Your countless miracles say You are; You are the one the prophets have written about for so many centuries. Snap the spikes! Break those shackles; silence the jeers! Come down from the cross!"

> SNAP THE SPIKES! BREAK THOSE SHACKLES; SILENCE THE JEERS! COME DOWN FROM THE CROSS!

Saint Mark saw it like this, as recorded in Mark 15:27–32:

> They crucified two rebels with him, one on his right and one on his left. Those who passed by hurled insults at him, shaking their heads and saying, "So! You who are going to destroy the temple and build it in three days, come down from the cross and save yourself!" In the same way the chief priests and the teachers of the law mocked him among themselves. "He saved others," they said, "but he can't save himself! Let this Messiah, this king of Israel, come down now from the cross, that we may see and believe." Those crucified with him also heaped insults on him.

Matthew sees it almost the exact same way (Matthew 27:38-44). And notice the intensity of the "Save Yourself" clan in Luke's Gospel, chapter 23:32–43:

> Two other men, both criminals, were also led out with him to be executed. When they came to the place called the Skull, they crucified him there, along with the criminals—one on his right, the other on his left. Jesus said, "Father, forgive them, for they do not know what they are doing." And they divided up his clothes by casting lots.
>
> The people stood watching, and the rulers even sneered at him. They said, "He saved others; let him save himself if he is God's Messiah, the Chosen One."
>
> The soldiers also came up and mocked him. They offered him wine vinegar and said, "If you are the king of the Jews, save yourself."
>
> There was a written notice above him, which read: THIS IS THE KING OF THE JEWS.
>
> One of the criminals who hung there hurled insults at him: "Aren't you the Messiah? Save yourself and us!" But the other criminal rebuked him. "Don't you fear God," he said, "since you are under the same sentence? We are punished justly, for we are getting what our deeds deserve. But this man has done nothing wrong." Then he said, "Jesus, remember me when you come into your kingdom." Jesus answered him, "Truly I tell you, today you will be with me in paradise."

Jesus was others-oriented, wasn't He? How do we know that? Reputation, sure. But look again at verse 35, at the sneering rulers. They're asking a logical question! Now put yourself back into that first-century scene. These people have gotten your brain a-spinning. You toss a quick, almost embarrassing glance down at your feet, pondering the jeerers—they really aren't too far off base. They make a good point. If He is who He claims to be, why doesn't He simply call it off?

#

Now, with the setting all in place, let's take the next few minutes to look back and see why Jesus couldn't respond to their demanding jeers and taunts and simply halt it all in its tracks.

There are four reasons for us to think about. Perhaps you can think of others, but for this reading within this time frame, four should suffice.

THERE ARE FOUR REASONS FOR US TO THINK ABOUT. PERHAPS YOU CAN THINK OF OTHERS, BUT FOR THIS READING WITHIN THIS TIME FRAME, FOUR SHOULD SUFFICE.

First, let's eliminate the obvious: modern archeology has uncovered many crucifixion sites. Research leaves us no doubt that the square nine-inch spike used to hold a person to the cross was the first and most obvious reason why He couldn't come down! It was the mere physics of the fastener holding the fastenee in place. Do some research of your own on the gory details; they aren't pleasant, but the specifics can fill you in on the background behind this first reason. But of course, it goes deeper than this.

Secondly, He couldn't come down because He was on a mission to fulfill Scripture. Both Matthew and Mark refer to accounts leading up to this scene and even marvelous discoveries made by the disciples themselves later, uncovering how much Scripture was being fulfilled by Jesus Himself. Remember how frequently we read in the Gospels the term "that the scripture might be fulfilled"?

Look at Matthew 26:53. Judas has brought his newfound buddies to the garden where Jesus is, and Peter takes his dagger out and swipes off the ear of Malchus, the servant of the high priest. However, Jesus, always others-oriented, bends down, picks up the severed ear, and restores it to the side of Malchus's head, all the while rebuking Peter because Peter doesn't really know the overall plan. And Jesus reminds him: "this must happen to fulfill scripture."

What is the "this" that Jesus is referring to—Malchus's ear? No, the cross is the "this" He's speaking of.

> JESUS KNEW HIS END; HE KNEW HIS DESTINY, YET HE DIDN'T FLEE TO THE HILLS. JESUS NEVER BECAME A FUGITIVE ON THE RUN.

Jesus knew His end; He knew His destiny, yet He didn't flee to the hills. Jesus never became a fugitive on the run.

Look at His words in Mark 14:49, the same scene where they've come to arrest Him: "I was daily with you in the temple teaching, and you took me not: but the Scriptures must be fulfilled."

Or how about the time in Matthew's Gospel, while in Jerusalem, that Jesus was teaching a great multitude through the use of parables and then ended with these words: "As you know, the Passover is two days away—and the Son of Man will be handed over to be crucified" (Matthew 26:2).

Thirdly, Jesus could not come down from the cross because it was finally His appointed time. Up until that point, no herd of stampeding camels, or stray arrow, or falling meteor could have accidentally taken Jesus's life; it wasn't His appointed time. Two things help to support this fact:

A. This fulfillment of Scripture made for the completion of His time. Psalm 22 is often considered the psalm with the view from the cross.

B. Jesus told His flock in John 10:18, "No man taketh my life from me, but I lay it down myself. I have the power to lay it

down and I have the power to take it again. This command-
ment have I received of my Father."

Look at the even more convincing words of Jesus in John 19:11
as He stands in front of Pontius Pilate. Pilate says, "Speakest thou not
unto me? Knowest thou not that I have the power to crucify thee,
and have power to release thee?" Jesus answers with the confidence of
the King of Kings: "Thou couldest have no power at all against me,
except it were given to thee from above: therefore he that delivereth
me unto thee hath the greater sin."

Could Jesus have died by any other cause? Could a runaway cart
have killed Him? Could a renegade herd of wild goats have gored
Him to death? Or a stray comet coincidentally bonk Him on the
head? Could Jesus have died before His appointed time? The answer
is quite simply no! Not with the eternal appointment that He had
scheduled on His "things to-do" list!

Fourth and most importantly (here's where you can breathe out
a PTL), Jesus had to stay on the cross to fulfill the mission that He
was sent to accomplish. What mission? The bearing of an enormous
burden. What burden? The burden of all sin, for all people, for all
time. A task that no mere mortal man could accomplish. Add to that
defeating the deceptive stranglehold that Satan had on the world ...
the stranglehold called death and eternity in hell. Somebody had to
do something about it, and it was this man who stepped up, raised
His hand, and said, "Send me in, Coach"—only to wind up nailed to
the cross, the one over there in the center.

Let's face it: we all know that Jesus could have snapped the spikes,
healed His own side, and tossed the crown of thorns onto Jupiter. Then
He could have just thrown up His hands and disgustedly said, "That's
it, folks, olly olly oxen free, let's all go home. I'm not doin' this cross
thing ... fend for yourselves. Father, let this cup pass from me."

In Matthew 26:53, Jesus asks His disciples, "Thinkest thou that
I cannot now pray to my Father, and he shall presently give me more
than twelve legions of angels?" (KJV)

But like the Good Shepherd who lays down His life for his sheep, Jesus endured the pain and suffering of the cross.

You could say that technically, He eventually did come down off there. Only to be placed in a tomb.

WITH THAT IN MIND, WE SHOULD NOT NEGLECT THE VIEW OF THE TOMB. IT IS THERE THAT OUR HOPE GETS NEW LIFE AND ARISES FROM THE FOG OF GLOOM AND ANGUISH.

The focus of this chapter began with a clear image of the cross, for we know that it is His body broken and His blood shed that have atoned for our iniquities. We therefore must also recognize that it was His shoulders on which the weight of our sins rested. With that in mind, we should not neglect the view of the tomb. It is there that our hope gets new life and arises from the fog of gloom and anguish.

It is the combination of the cross, where our sins are forever pinned, and the empty tomb, where our eternal hopes are majestically born, that gives rise to the renewed optimism of eternal life. We now can find rest in the peace of knowing that God has done the finishing work. He is truly the Author and Finisher of our faith.

Our hope comes from the resurrection; our peace comes from His Holy Spirit given to us; and our faith comes from the author of faith and Him who also gave us peace and hope through Jesus the Christ.

Today, we are permitted the opportunity of living in a time of knowing the glory of God's redemption plan for mankind. While the earth and its governmental systems remain under the control of Satan and His minions, it will only remain that way temporarily. We wait for the closing of escrow and the eventual transfer of the title deed of the earth back into God's hands.

The down payment, also known as earnest money, was deposited when Christ was born . . . when He bruised the heel of Satan.

However, the final purchase price was made on Calvary, some nineteen hundred and seventy or so years ago.

It simply behooves us to wait patiently for the paperwork to be completed!

The enemies of Jesus thought they were through with Him, that He was dead and gone—good riddance! They thought it was the end! However, in reality, it was only the beginning!

The tomb was not filled with death, but in fact bristled with Life!

Therefore, we know that physical spikes secured Him to the cross. Scripture prophesied that He was headed to the cross. Our sins sentenced Him to the cross. But it was God's love for us that

> OUR SINS SENTENCED HIM TO THE CROSS. BUT IT WAS GOD'S LOVE FOR US THAT LEFT HIM THERE ON THE CROSS!

left Him there on the cross! In the end, we are the reason He didn't come down!

#

To you who are looking on, the place called Golgotha, also known as the Hill of the Skull because of its unusual formation, has become the place of lost hope, despair, and misery. You are overcome with a sick sense of despondency deep in the core of your heart. Your soul aches as you look upon the innocence of this man who looks like He wouldn't hurt a fly. Dejected, your head slumps onto your chest, your hands plunge deep into your pockets, and your hopes dash against the jagged rocks of desolation. You instinctively kick a few pebbles out of your path as you begin to make your way from the place called Golgotha.

All the while, you are trying to block out the taunts of the blood-thirsty crowd.

One more time, as you near the edge of the hill, you glance back over your shoulder, one last, hopeful glance. To your dismay,

NO, HE WOULDN'T COME DOWN, AT LEAST NOT UNTIL HE KEPT HIS SCHEDULED APPOINTMENT WITH ETERNAL LIFE!

He is still hanging there. He hasn't come down. He won't come down.

If only you knew at that moment that you were looking upon God's ultimate redemption plan, established from before the universe was formed.

No, He wouldn't come down, at least not until He kept His scheduled appointment with eternal life!

"For God so loved the world that he gave his only begotten Son, that whosoever believes in Him shall not perish but have eternal life."

John 3:16 (KJV)

Marinating Moments

1. This chapter gives four reasons Jesus didn't come down from the cross. Can you think of other reasons?

2. If God has done so much for us, should we be doing anything for Him? Does He even expect us to be doing anything for Him?

3. Do you see the cross as a symbol of hope or failure? Why?

Marinade 13:

Our Advocate

"As it is written, There is none righteous, no, not one."

Romans 3:10 (KJV)

Erle Stanley Gardner, in all his years of great literary accomplishments, could never have written a Perry Mason plot quite as exciting as the one God has written for us.

Many times, Mr. Mason, the epitome of brilliant legal counsel, would be able to solve a murder scheme or larceny conspiracy chapters before anyone else could. Oftentimes the plots were complicated, tangled, and interwoven messes. At least, that's what we thought as we read them. The whodunits that we chose, based on the facts that we, the readers, were given, were oftentimes not the real culprits. Mason had a way, especially once in the courtroom, of exposing the dreaded murderer or conspirator by mere cross-examination. His way with words moved the reader from sheer confusion to logical triumphs. Gardner's clever stories capture the great courtroom drama.

The Bible tells us that there is coming a time when such courtroom action will again transpire. However, it won't be played out in a book or on television, but in a heavenly courtroom.

In the twinkling of an eye, you will find yourself seated at the defendant's table as the accused. Your defense attorney is seated next to you, waiting for His opportunity. He is actually patiently waiting for

IN THE TWINKLING OF AN EYE, YOU WILL FIND YOURSELF SEATED AT THE DEFENDANT'S TABLE AS THE ACCUSED. the prosecuting attorney to take a breather from his relentless attack on your character and behavior in your earthly life.

In the courtroom, there are only four present: the judge, the prosecutor, your advocate, and yourself. There is no jury to plead to, as this will be a trial by judge only. The courtroom is void of spectators, family, friends, news media, or court reporters.

As the trial begins, the prosecuting attorney will confidently stroll up to the judge's bench, sneering as he twirls the tips of his moustache, then arrogantly rubbing his hands together in that sinister manner that telegraphs his hidden agenda. Drool oozes out of the corners of his mouth as he recognizes you as a tender morsel of what we would call, in this situation, "dead meat." All the while, he continues to toss condemning glances and a crooked accusatory finger in your direction. Sometimes you get the feeling that his denunciations are really aimed at your advocate and are only hitting you with a glancing blow.

Propping one elbow on the judge's bench, the accuser glares at you. That sinking, jittery feeling begins to fill the bottom of your gut. Overwhelmed by his allegations and continued onslaught, you slink deeper in your seat. You are convinced that you are, in fact, guilty of all that he is accusing you of doing. Wagging his bony finger at you, he continues his tirade. His convincing and unrelenting tone has you so convinced of guilt that your sins have you fastened to your seat. You are ready to sentence yourself to outer darkness!

Point after poignant point, your guilt is unraveled before God. The prosecuting attorney glances at you, then back to the judge, then back to you repeatedly. You almost think you are at a tennis match.

Beads of sweat have coalesced and run down your forehead. You toss a couple of nervous glances at your defense attorney, noticing that He simply sits there quietly, checking out His fingernails, as He awaits his turn. He has no notes, no briefcase; He is only armed with a glow of confidence. He looks back at you with a smile and a reassuring wink. Somehow, you aren't so convinced that you are feeling reassured. After all, listen to the garbage you are being accused of! As if you really needed to acknowledge it.

POINT AFTER POIGNANT POINT, YOUR GUILT IS UNRAVELED BEFORE GOD. THE PROSECUTING ATTORNEY GLANCES AT YOU, THEN BACK TO THE JUDGE, THEN BACK TO YOU REPEATEDLY. YOU ALMOST THINK YOU ARE AT A TENNIS MATCH.

Sadly, it's all true.

Barely taking the time to inhale, the prosecutor continues to expose your sins. Your counsel just rolls His eyes.

Blow after damning blow, he reveals the continual failures of your life. In your mind, it's unquestionable that if he maintains this line of prosecution, you will be condemned for eternity, without chance of parole, without chance of defending yourself, in a dungeon so deep that you'll never see the sunlight again. You are thoroughly convinced that you sit guilty as accused. After all, he's developed an airtight case—perhaps the greatest slam-dunk case in judicial history. Back and forth the prosecutor paces the courtroom, raising his voice at the right times to accentuate the points he is making, flinging accusations and condemning reproaches your way, with your forever hanging in the balance.

BACK AND FORTH THE PROSECUTOR PACES THE COURTROOM, RAISING HIS VOICE AT THE RIGHT TIMES TO ACCENTUATE THE POINTS HE IS MAKING, FLINGING ACCUSATIONS AND CONDEMNING REPROACHES YOUR WAY, WITH YOUR FOREVER HANGING IN THE BALANCE.

Embarrassed, you sheepishly look around

the room to see if any of your family members might be there. They're not. They can't hear the accusations that you are being charged with. Besides, they've known what kind of person you are all your life. This is excessive and cruel, and you're not sure how much more of it you can bear.

Unmoving, your advocate patiently awaits His opportunity with the judge. He hasn't stirred; He hasn't attempted to jump up and object or move for a mistrial. In fact, He is still busy examining His fingernails, scraping a little dirt out from underneath the nail of His right index finger.

In a seemingly endless barrage, your accuser pounds ahead. Now even you are getting more bored than scared, as a slight yawn creases your lips. Eventually you start gathering the papers in front of you, stuffing your trial notes into a folder, prepping yourself for the bailiff to haul you away. As you prepare to accept your sentence to an eternal life of endless torture and darkness, a hopelessness that you have never experienced before begins to darken your heart.

But something's going on next door. There's a growing clamor of voices punctuated with angry outbursts and wailing.

Leaning over and whispering into the ear of your attorney, you bring to His attention that the annoying sounds in the next room are preventing your ability to fully concentrate on your case. With another comforting wink, and in an encouraging tone of voice, He reassures you that those in the other room are those who committed the ultimate crime: the rejection of Him.

As the prosecutor reveals solid evidence to the judge, your attorney begins to stir.

Finally, after a seeming lifetime of agonizing moments, the prosecutor's voice tails off on his closing and stinging statement: "And he calls himself a Christian!" He doesn't take his beady eyes off you as he makes his way back to his seat at the prosecutor's table.

The heavy silence hangs in the room like ocean fog hugs a coastline. The only sounds are the footfalls of an ant across the room, whose feet sound like drums pounding in a jungle.

Then, with cat-like swiftness, your advocate springs toward the judge's bench. He moves so quickly, in fact, that it startles you back to the present. He approaches the judge's bench without so much as a glance at the prosecutor, who sits smugly in is chair, arms crossed and a sinister smirk on his face.

In just a few words of His opening statement, your attorney begins to reestablish your credibility with the judge. His opening remarks in your defense go like this: "Dad, the person sitting at the defendant's table is truly guilty of everything the Prosecutor has mentioned; he is a bona fide sinner!"

Great, and He's *your* advocate—what a way to come to your defense! But swinging His open palm toward you, He continues. "However, several years ago he gave his heart and his life to Me. He placed his trust in Me and confessed Me to his friends. He eventually bore witness of Me to others in his life when he was baptized by water and by Your Spirit; he has been truly washed by the blood I shed on Calvary. It seems that his record shows no evidence of those sins. They have been expunged from his record, forever forgotten. Father, I therefore present to you a righteous man. Guilty of no sin. Washed by My blood. Represented by Me as counsel before You."

Turning toward you and tossing you a wink, He pivots back toward the judge and adds, "Therefore, as a result of his right standing before You, I recommend that he be allowed to enter into eternal life to worship and adore You from now throughout all of eternity."

As your advocate returns to His seat, a heavy silence hangs in the room once more. Both attorneys are seated. The judge reviews the evidence, occasionally taking a glance at the defendant. Seconds become minutes, which become centuries.

God, seated at the judgment seat, the Righteous Judge and the Judge of all, leans over the top of the bench and motions for your attorney to come closer.

"Son," He says, "because this man has received you as his Lord and Savior and has chosen to walk in the light and admonition of

> THEN, LOOKING AT YOU, GOD SAYS, "MY VERDICT IS THAT YOU ARE JUST. BECAUSE OF YOUR FAITH IN CHRIST, TRANSFERRING JESUS'S PURITY AND RIGHTEOUSNESS ONTO YOURSELF, I DECLARE YOU INNOCENT. YOU HAVE DONE WELL, MY GOOD AND FAITHFUL SERVANT.

our counsel, and because He has also chosen to follow My Word as it were a lamp unto his feet, I will not sentence him to be cast into the outer darkness, but rather accept him into My Kingdom as spotless as You. And, as far as the east is from the west, I will remember his sins no more!"

Then, looking at you, God says, "My verdict is that you are just. Because of your faith in Christ, transferring Jesus's purity and righteousness onto yourself, I declare you innocent. You have done well, My good and faithful servant. Since you have been faithful over a few things, I will make you ruler over many things. Enter now into the joy of the Lord, and welcome to the kingdom of heaven."

With your lower jaw stuck at half-mast, you realize that your attorney, Jesus, has just gotten you off the hook with the judge. All the accusations, all the condemning glares, all the damning, finger-pointing evidence flung at you by the prosecutor—they are not only forgiven but forgotten!

Standing, you reach to shake Jesus's hand. But He avoids your outstretched hand, and instead, with tears of joy filling His eyes, He envelops you with a huge hug. Arm in arm, you two begin to walk out.

Just then, the sound of the doors opening at the back of the courtroom attracts your attention. Someone else is entering; you aren't quite able to make out her face as she approaches. Your attention snaps back to the prosecutor as he stands up, sneering at the accused seated at the defendant's table. Jesus politely excuses Himself.

With an understanding nod, you release His arm as He heads back to the new defendant's side.

#

Whether the cases were developed by Erle Stanley Gardner's Perry Mason or Sir Arthur Conan Doyle's Sherlock Holmes, the answers were never so "elementary" to the readers. Engrossed in thought as we read their masterpieces, we were stuck in the mire of deducing the real culprits. We were often given information and clues relevant to resolving the crimes, but for one reason or another, we discarded or discounted them.

It is as true in life as in mystery novels: we are told all the facts, sprinkled throughout God's Word. Then it becomes our choice to accept the facts and solve the mystery of our lives through faith, or ignore them and forever suffer the consequences.

The mystery of the years has been revealed, as the apostle Paul writes to the Colossians in Colossians 1:26: "The mystery that has been kept hidden for ages and generations, but is now disclosed to the Lord's people."

> *"My little children, these things write I unto you, that you sin not. And if any man sin, we have an Advocate with the Father, Jesus Christ the righteous. And He is the propitiation for our sins; and not for ours only but also for the sins of the whole world."*
>
> 1 John 2:1–2 (NKJV)

Granted, this scene has been overdramatized. While it remains true that we will all face a certain judgment, it also remains true that those "in Christ" will only face what Paul calls in Greek the "bema" seat of Christ. This is the seat that Christ occupies as He metes out our rewards based on the works *for* Christ and the kingdom's sake that we performed in and through our lives.

> WE MAY CLAIM THAT THAT DOES NOT SOUND LIKE JUSTICE; HOWEVER, GOD HAS MADE IT CLEAR THROUGH HIS WORD—THROUGH THE PROPHETS, THROUGH THE GOSPELS AND EPISTLES—THAT THERE IS ONLY ONE WAY TO ETERNITY WITH HIM, AND THAT'S THROUGH JESUS THE CHRIST.

However, the noise in the other room, called the Great White Throne Judgment room, is the noise that rue and regret stir up as people come face-to-face with the fact that they are receiving their just reward for their rejection of Jesus as the Christ. Their good works, their giving to worthy causes, their years of clean living will mean nothing in the scope of eternity (Revelation 20:11–15).

We may claim that that does not sound like justice; however, God has made it clear through His Word—through the prophets, through the gospels and epistles—that there is only one way to eternity with Him, and that's through Jesus the Christ.

There may also be a third class of people: those who once walked with the Lord but fell away. We have heard of so many cases of people who have had a great relationship with the Lord at one time, but they became the self-appointed prosecutor and jury of their lives, sentencing themselves as unworthy to be called a son of god. The problem is they went one step too far . . . sentencing themselves!

The Bible encourages us to judge our own motivations, but it never says to pass the sentence . . . that's God's job.

In light of all this, where do you stand? Which room will you be led into? The one with the bema seat of Christ, or the one with the Great White Throne?

> *"I am the way, the truth, and the life. No one comes to the Father but by me."*

John 14:6 (NKJV)

"For it is written, As I live, saith the Lord, every knee shall bow to me, and every tongue shall confess to God."

Romans 14:11 (KJV)

"That at the name of Jesus every knee should bow, of things in heaven, and things in earth, and things under the earth; and that every tongue should confess that Jesus Chrsit is Lord, to the glory of God the Father."

Philippians 2:10–11 (KJV)

Marinating Moments

1. The great white throne room is the courtroom of ultimate destiny for those who did not give their hearts to Christ. What is your strategy to keep family and friends from that room?

2. Can you say, unequivocally, that you are destined for a hearing before the Bema seat of Christ? Explain why.

3. Think about what room you would be led to if you extravagantly shared from your abundance with your believing brothers and sisters in Christ or the church. Would that change anything? Why or why not?

Marinade 14:

The Hall of Hope

"Wherefore seeing we also are compassed about with so great a cloud of witnesses, let us lay aside every weight, and the sin which doth so easily beset us, and let us run with patience the race that is set before us."

Hebrews 12:1 (KJV)

Driving to the museum brought back so many memories of going there in Grandpa's car as a child. This time was extra special as I had *my* son in the passenger's seat, and this was going to be our first outing to the museum. We had visited the zoo, been to air shows, enjoyed early morning fishing excursions and so on, but we hadn't made this specific museum trip yet—for an explicit reason: timing. I had been waiting until Johnny Junior was eight to bring him here.

Timing was important, as there were going to be a number of things in the museum that I was going to have to explain to him, things that would be tough for an eight-year-old to understand if he were on his own. I was praying for supernatural guidance as I drove, all the while remembering my first trip here.

I remember vividly the day that Grandpa and I toured this very same Hall of Hope. It remains one of the highlights of my early years of life, and it stands as a marker, indeed a springboard, for things that God was going to do in my life afterward. Dad and I had our own

I WAS PRAYING FOR SUPER-
NATURAL GUIDANCE AS
I DROVE, ALL THE WHILE
REMEMBERING MY FIRST
TRIP HERE.

collection of adventures too, but after Grandma passed away, Grandpa took to spending more time with me.

Riding in his immense sedan was such a treat. It was always a thrill for me because over the years, it represented the opportunity for him and me to go explore the world, to share in new discoveries together, and to say that Grandpa and me were "adventure buddies." It wasn't long after he brought me to this particular museum that the Lord called him home to heaven.

I had never returned here since—until today.

Grandpa piloted the long, black cruiser of a car into the parking spot like a ship nestling alongside a pier and reached for the ignition switch to turn it off. As he did, he turned to me and said, "Johnny, I have waited to bring you to this museum for a long time. I think it's the right time now. I have been excited to do this, because there are things you are going to see in here that will have a profound effect on your life. I want you to feel free to ask me any questions that you may have. There are no questions too difficult for me to answer, and none too silly for you to ask."

He continued to look me straight in the eyes as he unbuckled his seatbelt. I reached for mine and began to press the release button when he reached over and said, "Remember, if you have any questions, or you see anything that specifically gets your attention, and you need me to help you to understand it—speak up, okay?"

I vividly remember the sincerity in his voice. In all our other adventures, he never spoke to me like that—with one exception.

It was that time when we were fishing in a boat on the lake and he became a bit concerned when I stood up to land a fish. I had reeled the fish up to the edge of the boat, and without waiting for Grandpa to get the net in the water, I yanked it straight up in the air to get it out of the water and into the boat. However, as the fish dangled from the tip of my pole, it kept swinging around in a circle. Neither grandpa nor I could grab it as it kept swirling in a big arc around the boat. The harder we tried to grab it, the more the boat would rock.

I VIVIDLY REMEMBER THE SINCERITY IN HIS VOICE. IN ALL OUR OTHER ADVENTURES, HE NEVER SPOKE TO ME LIKE THAT—WITH ONE EXCEPTION.

That's when I heard Grandpa's most serious voice on any of our adventures: "Johnny—stop and sit down!"

That's all he had to say. I looked directly at his face as he sat motionless on the seat. His look and his tone of voice were enough to bring peace to the situation and settle the rocking motion—and an unscheduled swim in the lake. Now, seated in the car, I heard that tone again.

After we entered the museum, Grandpa reached down and took hold of my hand. We walked in a few more steps, then turned left toward a door that had a sign hanging above it saying, "Special Display: The Hall of Hope. A Self-Guided Tour."

As we entered the Hall of Hope display room, it became instantly darker than the atrium we had just left. It took a few minutes for our eyes to adjust. Nevertheless, like film developing in a solution of chemicals, the objects in the darkness became clearer to my eyes as they adjusted.

The Hall of Hope was a long, narrow chamber. We stood on a carpet runner whose color I would describe as a royal purple with golden fringes. It ran the entire length of the room. The walls were covered with heavy black drapery, like the kind you would see hanging on a theater stage. There were no windows to allow natural light into the room. The only source of light came from downlights that were recessed in the ceiling, their beams individually focused on tall, white marble columns that lined the walkway on either side.

The columns were as tall as Grandpa and a bit taller than me. On each of the columns was the bust of a person, with an inscription just below each bust. It was one of the weirdest places Grandpa had ever taken me to.

As we walked forward, we stopped at the first column. This column didn't have a bust on it; it only had a commemorative plaque. Grandpa studied it for a bit and then read the inscription aloud:

> The Hall of Hope is a special touring display designed to encourage Hope and Faith in those who walk down the carpet of life. The characters that are represented in this room were never considered or construed as perfect, nor superhuman; they simply lived a life of Faith.
>
> "Faith," otherwise known as "Confidence in Divine Truths," is the foundation of things hoped for. Faith is the grounds on which we believe that God will fulfill His promises, even when we don't necessarily see the evidence.
>
> There may be stumbles and tumbles in every life, and not every event will seem positive in light of God's Word; however, God is ever present and assures us that, despite our failures, His plan for us is for good. He wants to use us, and this room is a demonstration of His Grace through our Faith.

Looking down at me, Grandpa asked, "What do you think of that?"

Honestly, I wasn't certain. So much of it seemed way over my head. "I'm not sure, Grandpa," I began in a muted tone. While there was no one else in the hall at the time, I still felt like I was in a library and needed to almost whisper.

"That's all right, Johnny, I didn't really expect you to understand that as it was written. So, allow me to explain. We are going to walk by a number of these columns here today. On top of each of them is a statue of a person who lived by faith according to God's promises.

And while they were not 'perfect' people, as the sign says, God wants to point out to us that He has a plan for each and every one of our lives, and that He is not looking for perfect people; He is merely looking for a person who is perfect for the task He has called them to perform. This room has on display those characters that God has used in the past, to encourage us to be used by Him in the present and in the future. You'll see what I mean in a few minutes. This will be like going through the Bible in one stroll down the hall."

Once again, he reached for my hand as he gave a small tug indicating that we were going to move forward. Stopping suddenly before reaching the next column, he looked down at me with that look that was becoming all too familiar on this trip and added, "There is a surprise at the end of the hall; I can't wait for you to see it. But we must work our way through these first." Then, not waiting for an answer from me, we began to move down the carpet.

We passed by a number of columns without really stopping at them, but Grandpa read some of the names aloud to me as we walked past.

"Here's one dedicated to the faith of Enoch, and this one is for Abel." We continued in a small but steady zigzag stroll, zigging from one side of the aisle and zagging back to the other side. "Ah, and this one is dedicated to Noah." He hesitated in his forward movement as he looked at me and asked, "Do you remember the story of Noah, Johnny?"

"Yes, Grandpa, he's the man who gathered all the animals together on his boat before a great flood came and killed everybody else, right?" I concluded with a somewhat guessing tone, hoping I got the right person.

"Yes, Johnny, that's good!" he commended me.

Our first stop was in front of a column that Grandpa said was the bust of Abraham. He preread the inscription and then read it aloud to me: "By faith Abraham, when he was called to go out into a place, obeyed and went out, not knowing where he was being called to by God." Grandpa paused and then said, "You know, Johnny, I would like to have faith like Abraham. Too often I have felt the tug of God on my heartstrings, but I didn't act on it. I think I have disappointed God on a number of occasions."

> "WHY, GRANDPA? IF YOU THOUGHT IT WAS GOD TUGGING, WHY DIDN'T YOU RESPOND?" I ASKED WITH DEEP CURIOSITY.

"Why, Grandpa? If you thought it was God tugging, why didn't you respond?" I asked with deep curiosity.

Looking at me with eyes that appeared to glisten from moisture, he said, "Because I think that at the time, there wasn't enough trust in my heart that it was Him calling me. Or I couldn't see the end, so I didn't want to take the first step. Johnny, I am not saying that my reaction was the right one. In fact, I have learned that it really was more a lack of faith than an act of faith, but these people here have taught me a lot."

Next to the Abraham column was one dedicated to Sarah, as Grandpa read, "Through faith Sarah was able to have a child, and that child had many children, more numerable than the stars of the sky and the sand by the sea. They all died in faith, not having received the promises, yet embracing the fact that the promises would be fulfilled by God!"

Looking down at me Grandpa said, "Man, that's real faith in God. Believing that God would provide a Messiah, yet it didn't happen in their lifetime. But God accounted them as members of the Hall of Hope because of their faith in His promises."

With the cluck of his tongue, we began to move forward again. We passed a number of columns before stopping once more. Pointing at the next bust and looking at me, he exclaimed, "Look who's on this one!"

I looked, but I couldn't read the inscription. I did notice that he had been carved with a different-looking hat or cap than the others. "Who is that?" I asked with genuine interest.

"It's Martin Luther. You want to know a man

LOOKING DOWN AT ME GRANDPA SAID, "MAN, THAT'S REAL FAITH IN GOD. BELIEVING THAT GOD WOULD PROVIDE A MESSIAH, YET IT DIDN'T HAPPEN IN THEIR LIFETIME. BUT GOD ACCOUNTED THEM AS MEMBERS OF THE HALL OF HOPE BECAUSE OF THEIR FAITH IN HIS PROMISES."

who really belongs to the Hall of Hope and Faith, it would be this man," he exclaimed. "You see Johnny, Martin Luther was the first in the organized church to boldly proclaim that salvation from our sins was through faith and faith alone. Not works, as had been so highly preached. He really had guts to take such a profound step in the face of the organized church! His act of faith set the church on its ear." He added a final thought, "You and I must look him up when we get home. His is a powerful story of faith."

With each column that we passed, time seemed to move forward. We strolled past some names that I didn't know, names like Whitefield, Henry, another named Spurgeon. I was starting to get bored.

When we reached the end of the columns, I was relieved to know that we were done. This had started out as an interesting adventure, but now it was monotonous. Just as I was about to ask if we could go home, Grandpa looked down at me. Then, kneeling down on one knee, he said, "There is one more room to enter. I promise you it won't take long, but I really want you to see it. Can you hang in there for a few more minutes?" I couldn't refuse an appeal like that from my Grandpa.

The columns ended, and the carpeted aisle made a ninety-degree turn into another room. This room wasn't a long hallway like the last one. It was a square about ten foot by ten foot. It still had the black drapes and the white illuminated marble column—just one. Curiously, this column didn't have a bust on it like the others.

We stood in front of the empty column. It was eerie at first. There was no statue on it, and I heard Grandpa sniffle a couple times. I looked up and noticed that he was struggling with his emotions. If I didn't know better, I would think he was crying.

"Why are we in this room with an empty column, Grandpa? Did they not finish the display?" I certainly sounded like an impatient child—but I guess that's what I was!

Turning toward me and again kneeling down to look at me on an even, eye-to-eye level, Grandpa took my face into his hands and looked directly into my eyes. With a soft and loving voice he said, "This column has your name on it. It is for your bust, Johnny. The plaque says: 'Because Johnny received Christ, by faith, as his Lord and Savior, Jesus has begun a good work in him; and because Jesus is the author of faith, he will complete it in Johnny.' My son, God has a plan for you. It is for good and not for evil. One day you will stand tall in the Hall of Hope!"

This time, Grandpa was not holding back the tears. He wrapped his arms around me and hugged me tightly as he sobbed a bit more.

"Why are you crying, Grandpa? Is this a bad thing?" I asked.

Through a few sniffles and a quick swipe of his nose, he looked at me and said, "Oh, Johnny, these are happy tears. Really, they are. I am so proud of you and what you're going to become."

"Does this mean that someday I will do something special for God, like all these other people did?" I asked through my confusion.

Wiping tears away, Grandpa began to regain

> THROUGH A FEW SNIFFLES AND A QUICK SWIPE OF HIS NOSE, HE LOOKED AT ME AND SAID, "OH, JOHNNY, THESE ARE HAPPY TEARS. REALLY, THEY ARE. I AM SO PROUD OF YOU AND WHAT YOU'RE GOING TO BECOME."

his composure. "Well, not necessarily, Johnny. God honors all who have shown faith in Him, even if they didn't do any great work other than merely sharing their faith through their lifestyles. Some He has called to do great works—some, like me, well, they didn't respond as well, yet He honors us all! Including me. Indeed, in spite of me."

"What does that mean, in spite of you?" I asked.

"Don't worry about that right now. Just live your faith, Johnny, and God will be well pleased with you. We are told in the Bible that we have this group of men and women of faith watching us. They have set the example of what it is like to run the race of faith. May you and I learn from them, Johnny. May we run the particular race of life that God has set before us, with patience and faith—and may we realize that He is running beside us."

#

I have fond memories of that day, and those memories had led me well through life. However, that was many years ago, and now it was my turn to bring Johnny Junior to the Hall of Hope.

The English ivy had grown steadily over the years, covering the stately red brick building substantially more than when Grandpa brought me here. However, the main entrance looked the same as I remembered it: bright, airy, and open. To our left was the door that had the familiar sign hanging over the lintel: "Special Display: The Hall of Hope. A Self-Guided Tour."

As we neared the doorway, I stopped and knelt down next to Johnny Junior and said, "There may be some things in there that may stir up some questions in your mind. Feel free to ask them. There are no questions that will be too tough for me to answer, and there are no silly questions. I want to make sure that you fully understand what we will be seeing here. Do you understand, Junior?" Funny, I used almost the exact words of Grandpa.

"Yes, Daddy, I understand. I will ask questions as they come up. Will this be boring?"

Uh-oh, I thought, *maybe I brought him here a little too early in his life. Well, we're here. May as well go in.*

As I remembered it, the room was narrow and dark, save for the spotlights focused on the white marble columns. The black, heavy drapery still hung on the walls, and the royal purple carpet with the golden fringes seemed like it was the same, yet it didn't appear to be any worse for the years of wear.

> I PAUSED, AS GRANDPA HAD, AT THE FIRST MARBLE COLUMN, REVIEWING THE INITIAL PLAQUE, AND READ IT ALOUD TO JUNIOR AS GRANDPA HAD DONE FOR ME.

I paused, as Grandpa had, at the first marble column, reviewing the initial plaque, and read it aloud to Junior as Grandpa had done for me.

"The Hall of Hope is a special touring display designed to encourage Hope and Faith in those who walk down the carpet of life … He wants to use us, and this room is a demonstration of His Grace through our Faith."

Reading that aloud to my son stirred a whole nest of emotions within me, including a flashback to the day Grandpa brought me here. As I remembered him crying, it seemed like only yesterday!

As we entered into the hall, we began to walk softly along the carpet, passing column after column. As Grandpa had done for me, I read to Junior the various plaques, starting with the ones proclaiming the faith of Abraham, Enoch, and Noah. Then I pointed out the busts of Jacob and Joseph, and I spent time on Moses.

"Moses was the one who got mad at the people, wasn't he, Daddy? Didn't he get upset and throw the tablets down and break them? Didn't God get mad at him for that? How come he's here? Isn't God mad, or did He forgive him?"

I was impressed with how well my son knew his Bible stories. "Well, that's a very good observation—and actually a good conclusion—on your part. Yes, God was upset with Moses, but He forgave him too, just as you remembered. That's true with God and us today. There are times when we don't lead a perfect life, and we do things that aren't in our best interest or in God's best

"SO YOU'RE SAYING THAT GOD LOVES US EVEN IF WE DO BAD THINGS?" JUNIOR ASKED IN THAT SWEET, INNOCENT VOICE.

plan for us. Nevertheless, God still loves us and cares for us, and He still cares about us."

"So you're saying that God loves us even if we do bad things?" Junior asked in that sweet, innocent voice.

"Yes, Junior, God does love us. God's love for us isn't based on our actions. It isn't based on anything we do. In fact, the Bible tells us that He loved us before we loved Him! That's pretty awesome isn't it?"

It was getting to be fun as I read about the different characters who were atop the columns. I passed through the Whitefields and the Spurgeons, I read to him about Martin Luther, and I shared about the movement Luther started on the basis of "faith alone," just as Grandpa had done for me. We were nearing the end of the display, and I spied the room that was at the end of the row, the room that Grandpa had taken me into to show me my column, when one of the last columns caught my eye—and I froze in place.

I know that Junior was momentarily worried about me, as he had never seen me sob as I did now. In all his life, he had only seen me tear up a couple of times, but this time it was more than he had ever experienced. I couldn't control myself as his little hand reached up and snuggled into mine. "What's wrong, Daddy?" came his sweet voice from below. "Why are you crying so hard? Are you scared?"

I looked down at him and then decided to pick him up in my arms. Regaining my composure a bit, and holding him tightly to my chest, I was able to direct his attention to the column that we were standing in front of, and I pointed to the bust atop the column.

"Junior, I'm going to read you this one too, okay?" I asked, not really wanting an answer.

"Okay, Daddy, read it to me," he said ever so tenderly as his little hand stroked the side of my face. Then he placed his little arms around my neck.

I began to read the inscription. "By faith, George believed that God would save his family and would do a mighty work in and through and by them. By faith, George prayed for his family regularly. He prayed that God would help them through life's battles and would keep them from harm; that God would spare them the fiery furnace and trials of life. By faith, George ran the good race and now sits at the feet of the Father."

My tears began a silent trek down my cheeks again, prompting Junior to ask in his gentle tone, "Why are you crying again, Daddy? You didn't cry at the other columns."

"Faith is not belief without proof, but trust without reservation."

D. ELTON TRUEBLOOD

Running my hands through Junior's hair, I smiled at him, sniffled, and then pointed to the bust on top of the column. "Junior, you see that man on the column?"

"Yes, Daddy, I see him."

"That man's name is George. He was my grandpa."

"Faith is not belief without proof, but trust without reservation."

D. Elton Trueblood

"And what more shall I say? I do not have time to tell about Gideon, Barak, Samson and Jephthah, about David and Samuel and the prophets, who through faith conquered

kingdoms, administered justice, and gained what was prom-
ised; who shut the mouths of lions, quenched the fury of the
flames, and escaped the edge of the sword; whose weakness was
turned to strength; and who became powerful in battle and
routed foreign armies."

Hebrews 11:32–34

Marinating Moments

1. Do you envision a column in the Hall of Hope with your bust on it? Why? Why not?

2. Fill in the ways God has worked in and through you. "By faith, _____ [your name here] _____ [fill in what God has done through you]."

3. What promises have you seen fulfilled in your life?

4. What weakness of yours has been turned into strength?

5. What answers to prayer do you recall? Reflect on your walk with Christ and record His great works in your life.

6. If you feel that your life has not exemplified faith to this point, I have good news! While these amazing men and women of faith have all completed their lives' journey, you and I have not. Therefore, we have a chance to write some more lines in our story of faith. What are some of the dreams our Lord has given you for the rest of your life? What daring ventures are there beyond your ability to accomplish? What is it that He is calling you to engage in? Write several lines of a faith-filled prospectus. By faith, [your name here] will ask God to help him/her dream big and get out of the boat! Take actions that reflect your belief that God is able to use an ordinary person like you.

Marinade 15:

We Like Sheep

"All we like sheep have gone astray; we have turned, every one, to his own way; and the Lord has laid on him the iniquity of us all."

Isaiah 53:6 (KJV)

As you drive along the scenic mountainous roads that wend their way through the rugged Gorges de Tarn in Southern France, you pass by many geographic formations that are reminiscent of Southern Utah in the United States. Huge flocks of sheep litter the hillsides. Mountainous terrain, beautiful glacier-cut valleys, and deep gorges etched out by winding and meandering rivers mark the landscape.

Along the drive, one particularly interesting sight is a solid piece of granite rock perched alongside of the road, called Le Sabot (French for "the Wooden Shoe"). Its shape is amazingly similar to that of the wooden clogs worn in Holland.

Continuing on, you arrive at a small town known the world over for its production of cheese. A tour of the naturally refrigerated caves here reveals thousands of foil-wrapped blocks of Roquefort cheese aging in seemingly miles' worth of curing racks.

Even more interesting than Le Sabot and more fascinating than the caves of Roquefort are the grottos of Aven Armand. Resembling the sights of Carlsbad Caverns in New Mexico or the Shasta Caverns

EVEN MORE INTERESTING THAN LE SABOT AND MORE FASCINATING THAN THE CAVES OF ROQUEFORT ARE THE GROTTOS OF AVEN ARMAND.

in Northern California, Aven Armand boasts of towering stalagmites, some over ninety feet high, which testify to the ages of the endless dripping of lime from their stalactite counterparts.

Slowly, by man's definition of time, drip by drip, these mighty subterranean formations have grown to monstrous proportions. Lying underground, undiscovered by man for centuries, the Aven Armand caverns laid in wait for an amazing and most unfortunate series of events.

Shifting gears radically, let's talk about sheep for a moment.

Sheep, you ask?

Believe it or not, they *do* have an important bearing on this story.

MANY OF THE CHARACTERISTICS OF SHEEP ARE WELL KNOWN TO MOST OF US. WE KNOW THAT SHEEP ARE BASICALLY STUPID. SHEEP ARE TERRIBLY DEPENDENT ON THEIR SHEPHERD FOR LEADERSHIP, FOR SAFETY, AND FOR FOOD.

Many of the characteristics of sheep are well known to most of us. We know that sheep are basically stupid. Sheep are terribly dependent on their shepherd for leadership, for safety, and for food. The shepherd guides them to greener pastures, protects them from hungry wolves, and tends to their needs. They feel absolutely safe in the presence of their shepherd and absolutely fearful when their shepherd is not around. So dependent are they on a strong leader that they will follow that leader anywhere, including off a cliff.

Which, incidentally, brings us back to the caverns at Aven Armand.

Before its official discovery, the pits of Aven Armand formulated events that terrifying legends are made of. Known throughout the countryside as the Devil's Throat, the region was renowned for swallowing travelers and herds alike.

One of the more colorful legends centers on a quiet, peaceful morning in 1897, when a flock of sheep helped to make one of the most exciting discoveries in Southern France. They didn't become famous by providing their wool for sale. And their fame wasn't because they provided Sunday diners with traditional, garlic-infused, fresh legs of lamb. No, they earned their fame by following their aimless four-legged leader to destruction.

You see, as the story goes, one of the sheep, who had been, unbeknownst to him, elected as leader, crept dangerously near the ledge of a gaping opening in the ground, subsequently lost his footing, and fell in.

A literal pit.

As the lead sheep fell, his flock followed. One after another, mutton after mutton, they all fell over the edge and collected into one huge wool ball at the bottom of the pit.

> AS THE LEAD SHEEP FELL, HIS FLOCK FOLLOWED. ONE AFTER ANOTHER, MUTTON AFTER MUTTON, THEY ALL FELL OVER THE EDGE AND COLLECTED INTO ONE HUGE WOOL BALL AT THE BOTTOM OF THE PIT.

Later that afternoon, the shepherd returned to the glade and began to hunt for his flock. They were nowhere in sight.

From a high vantage point on a nearby knoll, he spied the dark opening of the pit. He approached it cautiously. Edging up to the opening, he peered down into the chasm. All the while, he could hear the sounds of injured sheep bleating their groans of pain, and in sheep language, calling for help.

Unable to see anything in the black pit, the shepherd retrieved a rope and a lantern. Hastily he began to lower himself down, not knowing what he would find or what to expect. Foot by foot, he lowered himself deeper into the depths.

As his eyes began to adjust to the dimness of the pit, and as the lantern's faint light began to push back the darkness, he stared in disbelief as he saw his entire flock heaped in a pile on the floor of the cavern. The sight that caused him the most grief were the little lambs that had been impaled by the spears of the towering stalagmites.

Gored through their sides by daggers that were eons old, the flock lay helpless as life ebbed out, drip by drip. The shepherd dangled at the end of the tether, motionless, helpless, and weeping.

In despair he cried out, "Didn't you know that I was coming back to take care of you? Didn't you know that I was leading you to greener pastures, directing your paths? Wasn't it I who kept the wolves away? Don't you remember that it was I who left you to search for the one who was lost in the bush?"

Anguish dripped from every word. Impassioned sorrow ebbed from his heart to the victims.

The tragedy led to a major discovery in Southern France. Where for millennia the huge gaping hole in the ground rested in its solitude, the cavern has now become a huge tourist attraction, with guided tours into the bowels of the earth. To add to the attraction (and almost as an insult to the sheep), part of the tour takes you directly beneath the still exposed hole that the sheep fell through. Tourists pass directly below the original scene of the tragedy.

How easily we can relate human characteristics to those of sheep! Christians have a Shepherd, one who cares, one who wishes to direct our paths, one who wants to lead us by still waters, but more often than not, we choose to follow our own appointed or elected leaders, even to the point of falling through unknown pits and discovering unknown caverns. The treacherous spears that wait to impale us are in the hands of Satan himself.

Joshua said, "... Choose for yourself this day whom you will serve ... But, as for me and my house, we will serve the Lord" (Joshua 24:15).

We as humans are excellent at choosing leaders from among ourselves. We support rights that allow us the freedom to elect leaders. We will even fight to the death for those rights. However, there is a point where we allow human leadership to take the role of shepherd. When that happens, we become exposed, laid open raw, to the exploits and extortions of human leadership. Just as the lead sheep led the balance of the flock to slaughter, so will men, not filled with the Holy Spirit, lead other men to slaughter.

Jim Jones elevated his self-worth, his leadership role, to the point that nine hundred men, women, and sadly, children, drank poisoned Kool-Aid at his command. Jones rose to a power in his cult that could only be usurped by his supreme commander, Satan. The people followed him like sheep, even to the pit of Jonestown, and then straight into death.

Our shepherd, Jesus the Christ, loves us, cares for us, and wishes that none should perish. If we keep our eyes on Him, looking full into His wonderful face, He will protect us; He will guide us around the pits of certain doom and lead us into pastures green. Psalm 23 speaks of His green pastures and the quiet solitude that He guarantees there.

> THE IMMEDIATE DANGER COMES WHEN WE TAKE OUR EYES OFF JESUS, OUR SHEPHERD.

The immediate danger comes when we take our eyes off Jesus, our Shepherd.

When the apostle Peter confidently climbed out over the side of his boat to the surface of the sea, he was truly walking on water, looking directly at Jesus who was calling him. Once Peter looked down, he thought to himself, "What in the world am I doing? I'm not supposed to be able to walk on water!"

> HIS WORD CLEARLY WARNS US AWAY FROM SUCH ACTIONS.

At the very instant he took his eyes off Jesus, he began to float like a rock. He didn't just begin to slowly take on water like a foundering ship with a slow leak, but *ker-splash!* That is how quickly we can sink.

And we do not need to follow a cult leader like Jim Jones to begin wandering toward the pits of our culture.

When we go out of our way to drive to the theater, pay exorbitant admission fares for a seat and another outrageous charge for popcorn, and willingly expose ourselves to raw, blatant sin on the majestic silver screen, we are willfully taking our eyes off Jesus. His Word clearly warns us away from such actions.

And the pit widens.

When asked why church members were in the bar, the retort often comes back as, "I am witnessing to those people in there. They need to hear the gospel!"

The snare of the pit expands.

Have you ever walked along the curb, arms extended straight out for balance, trying not to slip on the newly planted grass seed while trying not to fall into the gutter of ankle-deep water? Then, all of a sudden, unexpectedly, your balance begins to waver; your body sways over the seedlings. And in an effort to recover your balance, you overcorrect and find yourself in ankle-deep gutter water. The solution would have been to either walk on the sidewalk, in safety and on solid footing, or in the street. Doing the Olympic balancing act on the curb is tantamount to playing with destruction.

> THERE ARE TOO MANY DANGERS THAT WALKING ON THE FENCE CAN CREATE.

Paul tells the Ephesians to "walk circumspectly" with the world (Ephesians 5:15, KJV). What does "circumspect" mean? It means to walk around the worldly ways, not on the fence. There are too many dangers that walking on the fence can create. Therefore, walking on one side or the other is safety.

But surely in the past you've been able to play the curb-balancing game without falling and getting wet or trampling on new growth. So, with the confidence of historically successful attempts, you try again.

That is Satan's game. You've played right into his hands. "Hey, look buddy," he whispers in your ear, "you can handle the garbage in this movie. It's realism, not that Walt Disney stuff."

He continues to plant thoughts in your mind. "Shucks, you're a well-rounded Christian, you can do all things. After all, doesn't Paul say that in the Bible?"

So convinced are you, that the new leader of the flock gets you to follow him into the pit. Only this pit doesn't have stalagmites and stalactites. It is virtually bottomless, and indeed very hot, and the moans of tortured sheep echo throughout.

Jesus said, "I am the good shepherd. The good shepherd gives His life for the sheep" (John 10:11, NKJV).

Jesus has already descended into the pit for us. He spent three days making a house call on our behalf. We don't need to resuffer the agony of death. He has done it once for us already.

Back on the highway, we emerge from the Massif Centrale mountain range, leaving the Gorges de Tarn, Roquefort, and the caverns at Aven Armand behind. Even so, we turn to our Good Shepherd to keep us out of the pit of hell.

"My people have been lost sheep; their shepherds have led them astray and caused them to roam on the mountains. They wandered over mountain and hill and forgot their own resting place."

Jeremiah 50:6

Marinating Moments

1. When have you pushed the envelope, knowingly crossing the lines of sin, but justifying it to yourself—"It's okay, I can handle it"?

2. This chapter urges us to keep our eyes fully fixed on Jesus's face. In practical terms, what does that look like? How do we keep our focus fully on Jesus in our day-by-day lives?

3. When have you seen others follow a human leader into dangerous places? What are the pitfalls of trusting other human beings to lead us?

Marinade 16:

Our Adversary

*"Be sober, be vigilant; because your adversary the devil, as a
roaring lion, walketh about, seeking whom he may devour."*

1 Peter 5:8 (KJV)

The star-studded canopy of night that draped the Serengeti Plains was
giving way to the rainbow hues that heralded the arrival of a new day.
Black faded into purple, which faded into light blues and iridescent
pinks. The sun began its slow ascent up Mount Kilimanjaro on the
eastern flank of the plains, chasing the stars off to the corners of the
western horizon.

It was a quiet, windless morning. The silence was only disturbed by the whistles of birds beginning their morning ritualis-
tic chant and the occasional chirp of a cricket, exhausted after a
night of calling out to fellow crickets. The grazing herd of gazelle
were unmoved by the screeching birds as they meandered along
the plains, enjoying their breakfast of savanna grass and tree leaves.
Struggling to crest the Kilimanjaro summit, like so many climb-
ers have done before, the sun took its position and flooded light
throughout the Serengeti.

Two hundred yards to the west of the herd, in the dry brush of
the tall themeda, otherwise known as red grass, despite the windless atmosphere, there was movement. The rustling of the brush was

THE RUSTLING OF THE BRUSH WAS SO SLIGHT AND IMPERCEPTIBLE THAT IT APPEARED TO BE UNNOTICED BY THE GRAZING HERD OF SEVERAL HUNDRED GAZELLE.

so slight and imperceptible that it appeared to be unnoticed by the grazing herd of several hundred gazelle.

Behind the disturbed themeda were eight sets of eyes peering out, observing the herd and devising a strategy for their own breakfast feast. The male lion lay virtually motionless, his tongue slightly hanging from his lower jaw as the fresh rays of sun glistened off his moist and jagged teeth. His tail maintained a slow but rhythmical up-and-down motion, quietly pounding at the soil beneath it. Pacing in front of him, and occasionally rubbing against his mane, the two lionesses impatiently awaited the command to deploy.

Without as much as a growl, the lion stood to his feet and pushed his head through the themeda. Then he turned and looked at the two lionesses that had stopped their agonizing pacing just long enough to receive the signal.

With experienced precision, the lionesses deployed into their tactical action plan. One headed to the north flank of the herd, remaining camouflaged by the tall dry grass that blended in well with her fur. She cleverly slinked in and out of the grass, to the rocks, and back to cover again. Maneuvering through the terrain, she maintained a watchful eye on the herd. Neither lioness wanted to make any sudden, distracting, or detectable motions.

The other lioness deployed south, on an ambush strategy. She, too, never lost eye contact with the herd. Finally, she stopped and stationed herself at a ninety-degree angle to her partner, who was two hundred yards to the north. They both stood on all fours, motionless, heads hanging slightly, panting to fill their lungs with as much oxygen as they could store in anticipation of the flurry of action that was only moments away. They both stood, just staring at the unsuspecting herd. They had mutually cast their crosshairs on several gazelle who were the closest to them—and farthest from the main herd.

THE OTHER LIONESS DEPLOYED SOUTH, ON AN AMBUSH STRATEGY. SHE, TOO, NEVER LOST EYE CONTACT WITH THE HERD.

Like an arrow being shot from a bow, the northernmost lioness darted out from her cover, exposing herself to the risk of antlers and hooves. Accelerating to full speed within moments of bolting from the camouflage, she had a few hundred yards to cover in full view of the herd. The further she could get before the entire herd was alerted, the better she would maintain the advantage of her preemptive strike. Her muscles bulged and strained with every grip of the soil beneath her powerful and deadly paws.

One gazelle, near the north end, but well within the herd, saw the lioness in full stride and darted in the opposite direction while others maintained a head-down position, chomping on savanna grass. Their stillness didn't last long. In a matter of moments, the adrenaline-saturated herd of gazelle was in full "fight or flight" mode—more in flight than in fight. Stampede!

The ones who were grazing closest to the prepositioned lionesses realized that they needed to bolt also, however, they were far away from the main herd by now, and they were not as swift as the others. Some were a bit gimpy, as if they'd been hurt. Some had scars and bruises that appeared to have been made by antlers and hooves. Others looked as if they had cat-claw scars on their backs and sides. They were no strangers to life on the Serengeti.

The southern lioness began her attack and broke cover at full stride. Like a team-roping competition, the two lionesses culled out one of the slower, weaker gazelles from the rest of the group and encircled it. One lioness, while in full stride, swatted at the neck of the gazelle, landing a powerful, striking blow to the head. She was moving so fast that she lost her balance and actually rolled away from the

ONE LIONESS, WHILE IN FULL STRIDE, SWATTED AT THE NECK OF THE GAZELLE, LANDING A POWERFUL, STRIKING BLOW TO THE HEAD. SHE WAS MOVING SO FAST THAT SHE LOST HER BALANCE AND ACTUALLY ROLLED AWAY FROM THE DAZED AND STUMBLING PREY.

dazed and stumbling prey. The other lioness took over by attacking the confused and bleeding gazelle from behind, pulling it to the ground. Within moments, both lionesses were done shopping and were coming home with their own breakfast.

Further south, the herd slowed down as they looked back to the café they had just abandoned, tables still littered with their breakfast remnants. But all they could see was one small cloud of dust that was beginning to settle, and within the dust cloud were the profiles of two lionesses dragging something heavy in their mouths back to the dry themeda brush from where they came.

Feeling a sense of safety, the herd was returning to normal. They were a safe distance from the attackers. Their adrenaline was steadying, and they were catching their collective breaths. Some decided to lie down to recover.

All was well again on the Serengeti Plains.

However, just a few hundred yards away to the south, the themeda brush was quivering in the breezeless morning sun.

"But if thou shalt indeed obey his voice, and do all that I speak;
then I will be an enemy unto thine enemies, and an adversary
unto thine adversaries."

Exodus 23:22 (KJV)

Marinating Moments

1. Perhaps images developed in your own mind regarding your-self and the "herd" as you read this chapter. Where are you in your walk with the Lord with respect to the herd?

2. There are times when we are wounded by those in the "herd," and there is a tendency to fall back. Has that happened to you? Are you safer, or in more peril, by separating yourself from the herd?

3. What would you say is the key to not becoming a victim of the adversary? What action steps should be taken to prevent our being eaten by the "roaming lion," our adversay?

Marinade 17:

Life Is But a Vapor:
A Young Boy's Story

"What is your life? You are a mist that appears for a little while and then vanishes."

James 4:14b

Along the timeline of human history lie dates of significance and importance in the development of mankind, times and events pinpointed by historians and chronologists as noteworthy in human history.

As you wade through the ankle-deep records of yesteryear, you discover midway through the twentieth century an obscure date, so insignificant to most that it precariously dangles off the edge and seems destined for the pit of obscurity.

That date? October 10, 1951.

In the overall scope of the dispensation of time, it is a meaningless and inconsequential date in a long line of boring and pointless times of humankind's existence. However, in the eternal eyes of God, it is as precious as any day in our collective story. Shuffle through an Internet search of this date on the timeline of historical dates, and you will uncover no significant event or consequential human birth that identifies it as earthshaking or of historical worthwhileness.

It isn't like many other days.

THE TIMELINE OF HISTORY
IS REPLETE WITH MEMO-
RABLE AND PROFOUNDLY
MEANINGFUL DATES. HOW-
EVER, OCTOBER 10, 1951 . . .
IS OBSCURE.

For instance, June 6, 1944, is historically known as D-Day.

December 7, 1941, is remembered as the attack on Pearl Harbor, Hawaii.

1492 is the year that Columbus sailed the ocean blue.

See what I mean? The timeline of history is replete with memorable and profoundly meaningful dates. However, October 10, 1951 … is obscure.

Except . . . to the scared, shaking, and lonely couple who were feeling isolated and alone in the cold, sterile maternity ward of a United States Army hospital in Western Europe on that day.

Follow along with me as I tell you a true story of what happened that fall day in the eastern town of West Germany as a newborn baby boy entered the world under the direst of conditions. When you finish reading this account, just put the book down, close your eyes, and reflect on what you've read. Think of how you would have handled this situation. What would be your thoughts? Moreover, how would you go through life afterward?

In 1951, the city of Regensburg was neatly tucked away in a remote section of a divided Germany, only miles from the post–World War II Czechoslovakian border. The American army had chosen to maintain a postwar presence in Europe to help balance an increasingly powerful and threatening Red Army representing the Communist Soviet Union.

Politics aside, the maternity ward of the hospital was abuzz with the normal activities of maternity wards: of delivering babies and tending to newborns, their mothers, and their nervous fathers.

However, for one stressed couple, this was not a normal day. It was anything *but* normal. Their newborn baby was in crisis. Fretting, they impatiently waited for the attending doctor's prognosis for their new arrival.

Shivering with feelings of emptiness and abandonment, the father paced while the mother lay in her postpartum recovery room bed. He wrestled with the idea that perhaps even God had forgotten about them and left them to commiserate over their dilemma.

Try as they might to repress the fears that the unknown creates, the parents of the child in crisis wondered within themselves, and aloud, about the outcome of the doctor's diagnosis. What was the depth of the trouble? What were the doctor's findings going to be? Was the baby going to survive—or not?

They were about to receive the answer to that question as the grim-faced doctor emerged from the neonatal intensive care unit. As calm and direct as he could be, the doctor informed them of the situation. The results of the complications during pregnancy and the traumatic birth meant that the baby boy had been challenged to receive the proper nourishment, nutrients, and a vital supply of oxygen to promote healthy fetal development. In essence, the baby's brain had been starved of oxygen for an indeterminate amount of time. In an extremely rare circumstance, it was surmised that, prior to the birth, the placenta had detached from the mother's uterine wall.

The vital umbilical connection between mother and child had separated during labor or some time before, which is usually considered too early for healthy fetal survival. The separation left the unborn baby lying in the womb, surrounded by fluids, unable to receive oxygen from the life-sustaining umbilical cord. The child had remained

THE VITAL UMBILICAL CONNECTION BETWEEN MOTHER AND CHILD HAD SEPARATED DURING LABOR OR SOME TIME BEFORE, WHICH IS USUALLY CON-SIDERED TOO EARLY FOR HEALTHY FETAL SURVIVAL.

suspended in a sea of amniotic fluid, his life hanging by a thread, unable to call upon his mother's reserves and unable to freely inhale oxygen as his needs dictated. Now, man could only stand by and watch. The fate of the child was squarely in the hands of God.

The consequences of a brain starved of oxygen can take a person down one of two lonely roads. Neither path is any more acceptable than the other. If the child were to survive the struggle and live, his parents should expect that he would need care in government institutions for brain-damaged children all his life. Perhaps, eventually, modern medicine could find a way to recover his lifeless brain cells.

The other road, which appeared to be the doctor's grim expectation, was death.

Some options!

Neither easily selectable.

> IT'S NOT LIKE THE PARENTS COULD SAY, "I CHOOSE WHAT'S BEHIND DOOR NUMBER 2." THEY SIMPLY HAD TO ACCEPT THE WAY THE CARDS PLAYED OUT.

It's not like the parents could say, "I choose what's behind door number 2." They simply had to accept the way the cards played out. There are some who call that fate. And some who call it kismet. However, God hadn't made His call yet. What happened next could only have been God's answer to man's lack of medical expertise or spiritual understanding.

Not wishing to helplessly stand around and just wait for the death of his son, and acting as if inspired, the father committed himself to searching the hospital for a man of the cloth, any cloth. Finding an army chaplain, the father explained the serious situation and requested that the baby be baptized before he died. However, a critical issue reared itself. After a brief inquiry into the parents' religious background, the chaplain regretted that he would be unable to perform the baptismal rite, as the marriage was not considered legal in the eyes of the denomination he represented. As it turned out, the father and mother were of different Christian denominations. This became a stumbling block for the chaplain.

Meanwhile, the dying baby lay in a life-sustaining incubator, virtually motionless, straining for every gasp of breath, destined to a life of being institutionalized at best. There was a chance that perhaps he would never get to know his original family. He would spend his whole life hand-fed by strangers he would come to call "family."

After an impassioned plea by the father, the chaplain reconsidered. The father had noted that, after all, the child's eternal life was at stake, and the baby was "non-denominational."

It took the strong reassurance from the attending physician that the child was perilously close to death before the chaplain would consent to performing the rite of baptism, with expediency—because with every exhaled breath, life was slowly ebbing from the struggling baby.

Within moments, the baptismal rite was complete. The parents' sigh of relief was heard throughout the hospital, and quite possibly, throughout the heavens.

The discussion of what to do with the child, if he survived, resumed. When the parents should be asking themselves what color they would paint his room, they were discussing what kind of institution to place him in. What effect would it have on his older sister? On the other hand, should we keep him at home and make some sort of effort to care for him ourselves or find help of some kind, maintaining the notion that perhaps future medical discoveries would lead to ways of recovering his damaged brain cells?

Questions intertwined among the emotions began to take a heavy toll on the couple. Grief mixed with hope blended with sorrow made for an exhausting recipe. This was their second child, but neither of the two had ever been faced with such despair.

Enter God!

> GOD'S DICTIONARY DOES NOT CONTAIN CERTAIN WORDS THAT WE SEEM TO USE A LOT, AND "COINCIDENTALLY" IS CERTAINLY ONE THAT WILL NOT BE FOUND.

God's dictionary does not contain certain words that we seem to use a lot, and "coincidentally" is certainly one that will not be found. However, it just so happened that coincidentally, one of the world's most renowned military neurosurgeons was touring military installations that week. And just as "coincidentally," he happened to arrive at this Regensburg facility within minutes of the conclusion of the baptismal ceremony.

The neurosurgeon entered the Regensburg maternity ward to the rush of swarming nurses and doctors. Instantly they recognized him and directed him to the still life lying in the incubator, sipping at breaths.

Eternity seemed like a drop in the bucket for the waiting staff. What were his findings going to be? How accurate were they in their own diagnosis? What would be the fate of the child? Thumbs up? Or the dreaded thumbs down?

After an interminable amount of time, about ten minutes, the surgeon emerged from his examination of the child. The staff was concerned, as his face was stoic and unreadable. There was no evidence of a verdict on his face.

While the doctor removed his sterile garb, he appeared to be deep in thought, as demonstrated by his quiet, determined demeanor. Then, turning to the staff and in crisp military protocol, he assured them that he was fully confident of their medical capabilities; however, it was his contention, drawing upon years of his medical schooling, years of practical experience, and years of neurosurgery, that the baby boy was destined for a life of normal activity. He had observed no signs or indications that the baby had suffered any brain loss as a result of the dire circumstances that had ushered him into the world.

"There appears to be nothing medically wrong with the boy, nothing wrong that a little time and nurturing won't cure," explained the neurosurgeon, to the delight of the staff and the parents alike.

The young boy left the hospital, and except for a condition called at that time a glass skull (where the skull bones haven't fully developed or thickened), he began to develop and mature into a typical little monster, as evidenced by the usual American family scenario: the frustrated mother and prematurely-grayed father. It was very clear to the new daddy that God had reached out and touched this young child as the chaplain presented him, and what was to be his life, to the graces of God.

In his later years, the young boy began to grow and develop into a mature young man. During his high school years he completed his confirmation classes while attending youth functions at the church. During one high school camp outing, the students were sent out into the forest for an "alone with God" time. Their task, upon returning to the campfire area, was to submit a question for the pastor to answer at the campfire or to pay the consequences: no dinner.

As I understand it, the young man was seeking the existence of God, so he wrote his question with a string attached. He asked that God would answer it in a special way. Later that evening, while singing around the campfire, the pastor began to read the submitted questions. However, the young boy's question, "If you ask God into your heart, how do you know He'll come in?", was not presented.

Dejected, and ready to conclude that God didn't exist after all, the young boy started back for his room when the pastor reached inside his sport coat and pulled out a piece of paper and recalled everyone back to the campfire. Before he read the question, the pastor addressed the group. "Now, for our last question, 'If you ask God into your heart, how do you know He'll come in?'" The young boy sat astonished; it was *his* question. The pastor continued, "I would like to answer this in a special way."

> GOD HAD INDEED MADE HIMSELF KNOWN TO THIS YOUNG BOY *IN A SPECIAL WAY.*

God had indeed made Himself known to this young boy *in a special way.*

Through the years, the boy continued to strengthen and mature. No signs of his rough beginnings were ever to manifest again, except when he tried out for high school football—being knocked out a few times by blows to the head meant that his desire to play NFL football would never be realized.

If this spared life was providence, the handiwork of God, then—why? Why did God do this? I have always heard that God has a plan for everyone. Did He have a plan for that young man? It should make you wonder, does He have a plan for you today?

Let's examine some evidence of this boy's life.

As a teen, he never lost the consciousness of the eternal presence of God. Even while serving two tours in Vietnam, he attended church services. Not always sure why, but knowing he needed to.

He was always compelled by and seemingly drawn to God and the Scriptures, as if they had become a part of his nature. In fact, in his older years, he came to know and understand that God had indeed planted His very nature within him. That healing touch of God meant more than physical health; it had implanted a way of life.

Shortly after his naval service ended, he found himself darkening the doorstep of a Calvary Chapel in Southern California. While there, he sat before a pastor named Chuck Smith, who profoundly affected his life through the exposition of Scripture and the demonstration of grace. The Word unfolded before his very soul, and the young man began to realize why God had done what He'd done for him. The young man was learning that God indeed had a plan, and now that he had made an adult commitment to Jesus Christ, it was time to dip his toes into the holy waters of spiritual service, to discover and develop the spiritual gifts he had been entrusted with, which had even been foreordained for him before the foundations of the world.

Before long he was hosting a home Bible study, which grew in attendance, but more importantly, grew the man. Year after year the desire for Bible study and the thirst for Bible knowledge were growing in him. All the while, God was patiently waiting for the young man to grow more in Him. However, there was more for him to do in his spiritual service development plan. God used him to develop the men's ministry at Calvary Chapel in Costa Mesa. What a journey! The highlight was the formation of a men's ministry program that grew throughout the Calvary Chapel ministries worldwide, capped by the men's conferences that were held, and continue to be held today, in the arena of the Anaheim Convention Center. As a result of the venue, he was able to share with and address as many as ten thousand men in attendance at these one-day conferences. He felt reassured that God could take him home to heaven, because he thought he had accomplished the goal that God had set for him. Later, he came to discover that this still wasn't the ultimate plan of God; he wasn't *there* yet in God's overall scheme for his life.

Feeling the familiar tug on that internal connection with God, he took his family to Oregon. He embarked on yet another new adventure, with all the associated twists and turns, as he laid the groundwork for a Calvary Chapel church plant. For ten years he grew spiritually, and the church grew in numbers.

However, after forty-plus years since that healing event occurred in Germany, it was finally becoming clear what God

HOWEVER, AFTER FORTY-PLUS YEARS SINCE THAT HEALING EVENT OCCURRED IN GERMANY, IT WAS FINALLY BECOMING CLEAR WHAT GOD HAD BEEN GROOMING HIM FOR.

had been grooming him for. As much as he loved to teach the Word, and as much as he enjoyed studying it, and as much as he loved to write, there was an aspect from *within* the Word that began to come to realization in himself and others around him. He felt that he had another function within God's plan, which was to groom and develop people for missions work. It became clear with the work that was being done in the postwar nation of Kosovo that he indeed was called to serve in the mission field. He was driven with the burning desire to take the Word and the message of the profound love of God to people who needed to hear it.

THAT BABY, ONCE DESTINED FOR A LIFE OF INSTITUTIONS AND DAILY MINISTRATIONS, NOW HOLDS A MASTER'S DEGREE IN COMMUNICATIONS FROM A MAJOR UNIVERSITY, HAS BECOME A PUBLISHED AUTHOR, AND SHOWS NO ILL EFFECTS FROM HIS DREADED MEDICAL PROGNOSIS.

That baby, once destined for a life of institutions and daily ministrations, now holds a master's degree in communications from a major university, has become a published author, and shows no ill effects from his dreaded medical prognosis.

In case you are wondering how I became so intimately acquainted with this saga, it's because I know that little boy very well.

In fact, *he grew up to write this book*!

#

All the symptoms were there. The baby who was supposed to be, best case, mentally impaired for the rest of his life, now holds a master's degree in communications. Not bad for a child whose doctor pronounced his destiny to be living the life of a vegetable!

I believe that on the day when God rested His healing touch on my hours-old, nearly lifeless body, He left an imprint. Much like a thermal imaging picture, there, impressed deep within my soul, remains the evidence of His healing touch. A spiritual thermal image, His handprint, is indeed still glowing red within me

ALL THE SYMPTOMS WERE THERE. THE BABY WHO WAS SUPPOSED TO BE, BEST CASE, MENTALLY IMPAIRED FOR THE REST OF HIS LIFE, NOW HOLDS A MASTER'S DEGREE IN COMMUNICATIONS. NOT BAD FOR A CHILD WHOSE DOCTOR PRONOUNCED HIS DESTINY TO BE LIVING THE LIFE OF A VEGETABLE!

and is an essential part of my very existence.

What does God have in store for me now? Is He done with me? Why do I still feel the ember of the spark He placed so deep in my soul? As I look at the many biblical characters, whom, when God had accomplished His plans through them, went home to be with Him, I find myself asking, will I be heading that way soon? Or are there other twists and turns yet to come in my life? Was that event that occurred so many human years ago, in a hospital so far away from here, all for what has been accomplished—or for what is yet to be accomplished?

The timeline of humanity's history stretches on into eternity, and history will continue to sift through those dates to determine worthwhile human events. However, along God's timeline, October 10, 1951, stands out. It was on that day that He brought and sustained life to a little newborn in Germany so that he could and would, eventually, come to know Jesus Christ as his Lord and Savior in a deeper, profound, and perhaps more appreciative way than many others have.

I believe there are days in your own history—your birthday, the day the Lord saved you, perhaps a miracle or work of protection He has done in your life—that are equally significant in His book.

I do have a number of questions, though:

1. Have I accomplished that for which God spared me?
2. Have I met the person or persons I have been foreordained to meet and influence?
3. Have I yet "apprehended" that for which God apprehended me?

I think the answer is D—all of the above!

As I mentioned earlier, it's time now to put the book down, close your eyes, and reflect on what you have just read. As you reflect on your life, think about the fact that God is obviously not done with you yet. How do I know that? Because He has allowed you to read this now! If He were done with you here, He'd have you next to Himself there!

We can't change the past. What's done is done. We can, though, change the present, which will affect the future—your future and perhaps the future of countless others. Like soldiers in the battlefield who jealously guard their ammunition, wanting to make every bullet count, are you making every breath you take count for Him?

So, I repeat the questions I asked at the beginning of the book: What really matters to you most in life? The shiny car? The big house? All those things that will rust or burn? Or the plan God has for your life, which may or may not include those material things?

Take a moment to look back on your life. The mere fact that you are even breathing means that God is not done with you yet on this earth.

Paul wrote to the Philippians in Philippians 3:12–14:

> Not that I have already obtained all this, or have already arrived at my goal, but I press on to take hold of that for which Christ Jesus took hold of me. Brothers and sisters, I do not consider myself yet to have taken hold of it. But

one thing I do: Forgetting what is behind and straining toward what is ahead, I press on toward the goal to win the prize for which God has called me heavenward in Christ Jesus.

I have looked at my life and asked, "Have I accomplished that for which God spared my life so many years ago? Or is that yet ahead of me?"

How about you? Have you fulfilled all that God has called you to do? Or is there more ahead of you? Ask Him and find out!

Never underestimate what God can *do* in and through your life!

Only one life, 'twill soon be past,
Only what's done for Christ will last.

Two little lines I heard one day,
Traveling along life's busy way;
Bringing conviction to my heart,
And from my mind would not depart;
Only one life, 'twill soon be past,
Only what's done for Christ will last.

Only one life, yes only one,
Soon will its fleeting hours be done;
Then, in "that day" my Lord to meet,
And stand before His Judgment seat;
Only one life, 'twill soon be past,
Only what's done for Christ will last.

Only one life, the still small voice,
Gently pleads for a better choice
Bidding me selfish aims to leave,
And to God's holy will to cleave;
Only one life, 'twill soon be past,
Only what's done for Christ will last.

Only one life, a few brief years,
Each with its burdens, hopes, and fears;
Each with its clays I must fulfill,
Living for self or in His will;
Only one life, 'twill soon be past,
Only what's done for Christ will last.

When this bright world would tempt me sore,
When Satan would a victory score;
When self would seek to have its way,
Then help me Lord with joy to say;
Only one life, 'twill soon be past,
Only what's done for Christ will last.

Give me Father, a purpose deep,
In joy or sorrow Thy word to keep;
Faithful and true what e'er the strife,
Pleasing Thee in my daily life;
Only one life, 'twill soon be past,
Only what's done for Christ will last.

Oh let my love with fervor burn,
And from the world now let me turn;
Living for Thee, and Thee alone,
Bringing Thee pleasure on Thy throne;
Only one life, 'twill soon be past,
Only what's done for Christ will last.

Only one life, yes only one,
Now let me say, "Thy will be done";
And when at last I'll hear the call,
I know I'll say "'twas worth it all";
Only one life, 'twill soon be past,
Only what's done for Christ will last.

Only one life, 'twill soon be past,
Only what's done for Christ will last.
And when I am dying, how happy I'll be,
If the lamp of my life has been burned out for Thee.
(C.T. Studd)

Marinating Moments

1. Someone has said, "You haven't lived until you've nearly died." What do you think of that statement? Knowing that your life along the timeline of human history is but a mist or a vapor, what is your focus in life?

2. What changes could you make today to accomplish God's will and His plans for your life?

3. Like a soldier on the battlefield, not wishing to waste any bullets, have you made every breath of your life count for the kingdom's sake?

4. What I find reassuring is that, despite my failures, my stumbles through life, God has always picked me up, dusted me off, and placed me back in service. Has God done that for you? How many times? What does it mean to you that His grace would go so far as to place you in His marvelous plans?

5. Have you yet apprehended that for which you were apprehended?

6. If this were the start of your life, how would it affect the way you see your life? What would be your thoughts about it? Moreover, how would you go through life?

Connect with the Author:

Website: MarinatingMoments.com

E-Mail: MarinatingMoments@gmail.com